TRADITIONAL COUNTRY LIFE REC

APPLE
COMPANION

TRADITIONAL COUNTRY LIFE RECIPE SERIES

APPLE COMPANION

Recipes by
Liz Clark

Apple Consultant
Jill Vorbeck

Interior Illustrations   *Cover Illustration*
Alison Gail   Lisa Adams

The Brick Tower Press ®
1230 Park Avenue, New York, NY 10128
Copyright © 1994
Liz Clark & Jill Vorbeck

Clark, Liz
Vorbeck, Jill
The Traditional Country Life Recipe Series:
Includes Index
ISBN 1-883283-05-1 softcover

Library of Congress Catalog Card
Number: 94-78780
First Edition, October 1994
Second Edition, September 1995

TABLE OF CONTENTS

Apple Facts...2

Beverages...22

Appetizers...24

Soups...30

Breakfast...34

Applesauce...37

Main Dishes...39

Vegetables...58

Salads ...62

Breads & Muffins...65

Desserts...78

Vinegars & Jellies...101

Index...106

EATING APPLES

There may be thousands of varieties, but to cooks, all apples are divided into two kinds: "cooking apples" and "eating apples." The presentation of "eating apples" can be as utterly simple as a brief pause for a shirt-rub polishing between branch and tooth on a brisk autumn day in the orchard, or it can be as formal as an elegant continental fruit and cheese dessert by candlelight. One of my happiest dining memories is a simple dessert of whole Jonalicious apples, aged cheddar cheese, homemade French bread, and whole English walnuts offered on a grape leaf-lined tray. Everyone lingered at the table for hours nibbling and talking in the warm glow of friendship.

On the informal side, "eating apples" are the traditional brown bag lunch dessert, equally welcome in school, factory, and office. A bag of fresh-picked apples nourishes many a farmer in the cab of his combine through the long hours of harvest. Crisp, whole fresh apples fit naturally into most traditional autumn outdoor activities: bicycling tours, fall-color hikes, Halloween bonfires with scary ghost stories, homecoming games. Offhand, I can recall only one occasion where apples didn't "work." The year our fruit trees bore their first crop, we took a canoe trip into the Boundary Waters Canoe Area. Before the trip, nobody could persuade my husband, Tom, that it was not a good idea to take along a bushel of the first fruits from his young orchard. It took only a few portages to convince even the proud grower that 40 pounds of "snack food" was not appropriate for a back-packing adventure!

Any weekend visitor to our farm has come to expect at least one "apple tasting meal." We're always trying new varieties and are eager to evaluate their quality, so we enlist guests to participate in taste tests. The meal consists of fresh homemade French bread, cheddar cheese, butter, and about six different varieties of apples. Occasionally, I still serve soup before, or an apple dessert after, this menu. But with experience, I've learned that the bread, cheese, and apples constitute a full meal, and any other dish is really superfluous.

What variety is the best "eating apple"? For fresh eating, most folks prefer a flavor that tilts to the sweet side of the sweet-tart balance. Most demand crisp texture. When you try taste testing a few apple varieties with a group you'll instantly learn there is no unanimous choice. The flavor that lifts your feet off the ground might be judged mediocre by some or disliked even more by others.

The *National Apple Register of the United Kingdom*, published in 1971, lists over 6,000 names of apple varieties grown in Great Britain over the period 1853-1968. Surely hundreds of new varieties have been introduced around the world since. Imagine that if cloning of human beings had been possible centuries ago, the world today would be populated by many copies of departed greats like Socrates, Shakespeare, and Einstein. Since cloning has been practiced on apples since the days of ancient Rome, outstanding varieties from centuries past are still being grown today.

Every variety you find in the market or in a nursery catalog has been thoroughly screened. For an apple variety to survive hundreds of years and be here today, it had to be preferred by generations of nurserymen. A modern apple breeder will test thousands of seedlings before introducing one new variety, and before introducing and promoting a new variety, a nursery must be convinced it is superior in some quality to any other variety on the market.

As you try different apple varieties, keep a log of your preferences so you'll know what to look for next week or next year. As you taste, keep in mind that the intense apple you savor with cheese on special occasions is different from the apple you choose for lunch every day.

THE ANTIQUE APPLE MYSTIQUE

Usually the term "antique" is applied to apple varieties widely cultivated over 100 years ago that are not grown commercially today. Many of today's leading commercial varieties qualify as antiques based on age alone. Red Delicious originated around 1880, Golden Delicious in 1890. Jonathan has been around since 1826, McIntosh since 1796, and Rome Beauty since 1848. The term "antique" is not used for these varieties that have beat the competition and stayed popular. "Antique" is reserved for the ones that dropped into obscurity. Why then did many antique apples disappear from orchards?

A whole way of life changed. Both sets of my own grandparents were farmers. My husband Tom's great-great-grandfather homesteaded the farm where we live today. When we decided to move to the farm, Tom's Mom was especially delighted that we might reestablish the small home orchard she remembered from her childhood. Like most farmers two generations ago, our grandparents grew their own fruits and vegetables, and produced their own meat and eggs.

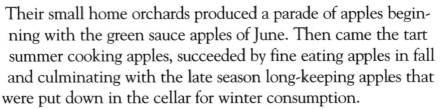

Their small home orchards produced a parade of apples beginning with the green sauce apples of June. Then came the tart summer cooking apples, succeeded by fine eating apples in fall and culminating with the late season long-keeping apples that were put down in the cellar for winter consumption.

Meanwhile, some varieties were dried or pressed into cider, while others were cooked, turned into applesauce or apple butter, sealed in quart jars and stocked in the cellar shelves.

It was a slower paced, simpler time when the flavor of apples rated serious consideration. The apple varieties were different, but the apples were grown near at hand, tree-ripened, and people had the time, desire, skills, and the tools to process them. Home-grown fresh apples were an important part of the diet and routinely used in a wide variety of dishes.

When we mourn the loss of old varieties, we need to recall the context of the world when they were grown. A few cooks still long for the old, now hard to find, Yellow Transparent apple for summer applesauce. But the great majority never have, and never will, make applesauce. When the demand for summer sauce-apples disappeared, most apple growers stopped growing them.

This is just one example from hundreds why a particular variety, once common, dropped out of production and became an "antique." Refrigeration and controlled atmosphere storage spelled the end to some old varieties. Most folks just don't store their winter supply of apples in the unheated fruit cellar anymore (another endangered species!) As a result the demand for those old-time keeper apples such as Arkansas Black, Willow Twig, and Ben Davis disappeared.

As apples are sensitive to slight climate variations, an apple that is excellent in one region is mediocre or worse in another. The ascent of nationwide supermarket chains and mass distribution systems spelled the demise of many regional favorites that were never grown outside a limited geographical area.

Some good tasting varieties were unprofitable because they were disease-prone or shy bearers or yielded fruit every two years. Some were too small or too ugly to appeal to a generation accustomed to shiny red, blemish-free apples as the standard of excellence. Some of the antiques that disappeared from cultivation were displaced by newer introductions with superior qualities.

The supermarket with its year-round display of the same few "commercial" varieties belies the fact that the apple is a seasonal fruit. Just as you never find a tree-ripened white peach or nectarine in the supermarket, some apples are too fragile or perishable to reach grocery store shelves, like Chenango Strawberry and the tender Spigold.

Are the old varieties in danger of extinction? Although most of the "antique" apples will continue to be about as rare as dinosaurs on supermarket shelves, they are not "extinct." Specialty nurseries continue to propagate antique apples. The 1992 Seed Savers Exchange publication called *Fruit, Berry and Nut Inventory - Second Edition*, lists 1,180 apple varieties sold by U.S. nurseries. Specialty apple growers across the country continue to grow and sell antique apples of merit.

Flavor intensity is one trait many antiques share -- something only a small percentage of the population values. This trait is rare in modern apples, but anyone looking for intensity should look not only to the venerable antiques (such as Ashmead's

Kernels, Golden Russets, and Newtown Pippins), but also to modern apples like Freyburg and Gold Rush.

If you want outstanding apples, scout your area's orchards, farmers markets, and roadside stands for growers who care about flavor. Be open minded enough to try what they recommend. If you have your heart set on an antique, you just might miss trying a new variety that's ten times better! If you want better flavor, don't insist on moving back to inferior varieties but move to the best - whether old or new.

THE "SMITH MYTH"

Is Granny Smith the best apple for cooking? Most experts agree that a great cooking apple has high sugar content and high acid content and holds its shape when cooked until tender. Granny meets these criteria - along with hundreds of other apple varieties. Granny is very productive and has characteristics that allow growers to manipulate it in cold storage to retain high quality 12 months of the year. These qualities make Granny a unique apple.

The Smith Myth upsets me for two reasons: First, the growing season here in the mid-west (like most of the rest of the US) is too short to ripen the long season Granny in most years. Anyone following a published recipe calling for Granny Smith might think they can't cook with locally grown apples, but only with Granny's shipped in from Washington, California, or the southern hemisphere. Second, I favor diversity and Granny, fine as she can be, just doesn't deserve to push all the other great cooking apples out of the marketplace.

Still, I do understand and even sympathize with, the reasons recipe developers concentrate on Granny Smith. I've asked variety collectors across the country, "What is the best cooking apple?" As they talk, the answers eventually fall into this pattern: "Well, I start out in early summer with 'A,' then go to 'B' and 'C,' and put away a bushel each of 'X' and 'Y' and 'Z' for winter baking." The experts are still cooking the way our ancesters did - not with one cooking variety - but with a succession of at least half a dozen through the harvest season - and the list changes in each area of the country!

This is not the sort of advice a food writer can incorporate in an everyday apple recipe for a nationwide audience! Since Granny Smith is the one cooking apple likely to be available in all parts of the country every day of the year, it has become the recipe writers' shorthand for a "good cooking apple."

If you have to buy your cooking apples in a supermarket, a good Granny Smith may be your best choice most of the time. But please don't abandon all the other great cooking apples - old and new - for the comfort of the ubiquitous Granny! Even in grocery stores, other widely available varieties - Golden Delicious, Idared, and Braeburn to name just a few - would be better choices than immature rock-hard Granny's.

COOKING APPLES

Rather than limiting your horizons by recommending a single variety for each of Liz's luscious recipes, I've compiled lists of great cooking apples for applesauce, salads, main dishes, and desserts. These are starting points only. Experiment with any cooking apples you find and keep a log of your successes. You'll soon have your own personalized "Expert's List" of excellent cooking apples.

APPLESAUCE

Most people like an apple that cooks down quickly for a smooth applesauce. Traditional early summer favorites are Yellow Transparent and Red Astrakhan. The pink-fleshed apples, such as Almata and Pink Pearl, make an interesting pink-colored sauce. Aromatic apples like McIntosh, Sir Prize, and Priscilla are mentioned as the top choices of variety collectors.

Our own best applesauce has been a byproduct from large apple tasting events. We toss any "leftover" cut apples in a big pot and add enough fresh cider to start the cooking down process. We cook and stir until the apples are soft enough to run through the food mill. Combining several apple varieties produces a rich, complex sauce that needs no sugar or spice added to it. Sweet, juicy, apples like Golden Delicious and Jonagold make wonderful unsweetened applesauce.

SALAD

Here is an area where great "eating apples" and "cooking apples" overlap! Your favorite eating apples will add crunch and sweetness to green salads.

The most delightful revelation for me in Liz's September apple menu, is the flavor Marriage-Made-In-Heaven between the anise flavor of the Freyburg apple and the pungent blue cheese in her stunning "Baby Garden Green Salad/Blue Cheese/Apple and Red Onion." (see page 63) Another anise-flavored apple to try in salads is Sweet Sixteen.

Two traditional favorite "salad apples" are the sweet Golden Delicious, and tart Cortland, both noted for non-oxidizing flesh - i.e. the flesh will stay white rather than turning brown soon after being cut. Other varieties highly recommended by collectors were Gala, Fuji, and Mutsu.

MAIN DISHES

Look for apples with a rich, tart, assertive flavor. Avoid mild or sweet apples that would be overpowered by other flavors. Some suggestions: Melrose, Jonathan, Idared, Monark, Braeburn, Gold Rush, Winesap, Calville Blanc, Northern Spy, Gravenstein, Cortland, Granny Smith, Pink Pearl. Also try any other tart apple from the "Desserts" list.

Where Liz calls for "red skinned" apples in main dish recipes, she is looking for the aesthetic contrast of the red skin and white flesh of the apple. There is no implied correlation of flavor with color.

DESSERTS

Here is a list of varieties recommended by apple variety collectors:

Sweet Apples

Fuji
Gala
Golden Delicious
Honey Gold
Jonagold
Mutsu

Tart Apples

Belle de Boskoop	Monark
Bramley's Seedling	Newtown Pippin
Calville Blanc	Northern Spy
Cortland	Prima
Granny Smith	Rhode Island Greening
Grimes Golden	Signe Tillich
Idared	Spartan
Jonathan	Spigold
McIntosh	Summer Rambo
Melrose	Winesap

Most apple dessert recipes are developed and tested using tart apples. Sweet apples are used successfully in desserts, but only if the amount of sugar is drastically reduced.

Many thanks to the apple experts who shared their wisdom and variety recommendations: Grady Auvil, Thomas Burford, Connie Doud, Ed Fackler, Mike Janket, Walda Janson, Robert Nitschke, and Tom Vorbeck.

APPLE TACKLE

The five pieces of apple tackle described below greatly ease the job of tackling any apple recipe using whole, fresh apples instead of something from a can. The two most essential apple tools are a sharp paring knife and a good knee-action vegetable peeler. But if you have even a single apple tree in your yard (or have access to a good farmer's market, orchard, or roadside stand), you will love having efficient Apple Tackle in your kitchen!

APPLE PEELER/CORER/SLICER
(HEREAFTER CALLED "THE MACHINE")

"Peel, core, and slice." Those four little words need never again cause you to hesitate to tackle an apple recipe - with vacuum-based apple peeler/corer/slicer machines, the formerly onerous task of turning fresh apples into pie tinder becomes a joy. And it's not just for pies. This wonderfully versatile machine shortcuts the labor for countless apple preparations.

First attach the clean vacuum base to any smooth clean countertop. I usually attach my machine to my antique porcelain topped Hoosier cabinet. It also works great with Formica and glass, but if your countertops are bumpy, buy a smooth Formica "sink-cutout" from a hardware store or cabinet maker to use with vacuum-based appliances. Release the spring lever and pull the shaft all the way to the right. Impale a fresh apple firmly, stem end first, on the three-pronged fork then, holding the spring lever down, advance the shaft until the surface of the apple touches the peeling blade. Now release the spring lever and turn the handle. As the rotating shaft turns the apple, the peeling blade will shave off the peel in one continuous strip while the corer-slicer blade removes the central cylinder of core and carves the flesh into a spiral. Keep turning the handle until the apple completely clears the corer-slicer blade. Remove the apple and set it on a cutting board. Release the spring lever and retract the shaft to its starting position. Usually, the corer-slicer blade will smartly pop the cylinder of apple core off the three-pronged fork as you do this (one of life's little joys!). I mount the machine near the front edge of the countertop and set my compost bucket on the floor between my feet and the counter and let the peel feed directly into it then sweep the cores in as they pop off the prongs.

Occasionally, a core stubbornly squeezes back through the circular coring blade and you'll have to pry it off the prongs by hand (sigh). This all happens faster than you can read about it. Take a paring knife and cut a radius through the apple spiral to form rings. Cut the rings in half for rainbow-shaped slices. With a little practice, you can peel, core, and slice enough apples to fill a pie in five minutes.

The machine works best with fresh, crisp, round, not-too-large apples with a centered core. Fortunately, it's a perfect match with Jonathan, my own favorite pie apple! If the apples you are using don't fit this description, you can still use the machine to great advantage.

Three-pronged fork

Shaft

Corer-slicer Blade

Peeling Blade

Peeling Arm

Lopsided apples, and apples that are too large or too firm to feed through the slicing blade, can still be peeled on the machine. Loosen the wing-nut at the front of the machine with a pair of pliers and drop the corer-slicer blade out of the way. Then follow the procedure above to peel the whole apple, although you will have to remove the whole peeled apple from the three-pronged fork manually (sigh).

Even with perfect apples, you might choose the peel-only function of the peeling machine for flexibility in slicing. Use the other tools we describe below in combination with the peeler/corer/slicer machine for the greatest efficiency and versatility. Core a whole peeled apple with the apple corer for whole baked apples. Use the corer-wedger to divide a whole peeled apple into ten uniform wedges for recipes where you want thick slices. Use the pear corer to quickly core peeled apple halves or quarters.

Peel

You can also core and slice apples without peeling. Pull back the peeling arm and flip the little metal lock lever to wedge it out of the way. The thin rings with the peeling attached are popular with children. It's fun to watch the machine work and the rings are somehow more exotic and appealing than ordinary, everyday whole apples. The spiral with peeling intact can be used in many of Liz's recipes. Cut a red-skinned spiral with the corer-wedger for tiny red-rimmed ring-segments, perfect for salads, poultry stuffing, etc.

To reset the coring and slicing blade, lift it back up to its approximate position then push the shaft all the way through the hole that cores the apple. Make sure the blade is properly aligned by stopping the widest part of the pronged fork inside the coring hole. Tighten the wing nut that holds the coring blade while the machine is in this position.

You can also adjust the thickness of the peeling by the distance the U-shaped peeling blade sets out from the peeling arm. The less air you see between the blade and the arm, the thinner the peeling. If the machine peels too deeply, loosen the wing nut and move the peeling blade closer. If you try to cut too thin a peel, the machine is likely to skip since no apple is perfectly smooth and round. I set the peeling blade at the slightest angle toward the handle rather than square with the horseshoe shaped guide on the peeling arm. Experiment!

With most apple varieties, you'll only be able to use the machine in the fall while the apples are still fresh and firm. It does not work well with overripe, soft apples. With practice, you can learn to reduce the pressure a bit on the peeling arm by holding it back with your left thumb to allow you to peel softer apples. After most varieties are long past being machine-peelable, a few exceptionally good keepers (such as Fuji, Granny Smith, Newtown Pippin, Stayman Winesap, Arkansas Black, and Gold Rush) will hold their firm texture. But most apple varieties will simply not be machine peelable after January. Outside the harvest season, experiment with any firm apples available to you, but if the machine won't work, don't be frustrated and think you're doing something wrong. Wait until fall and bring out the machine for the new crop of fresh firm apples.

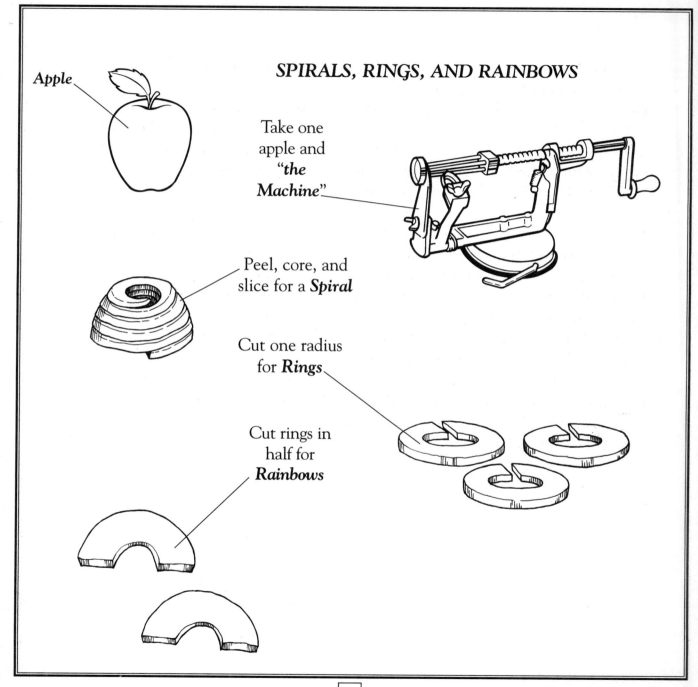

SPIRALS, RINGS, AND RAINBOWS

Apple

Take one apple and **"the Machine"**

Peel, core, and slice for a **Spiral**

Cut one radius for **Rings**

Cut rings in half for **Rainbows**

THE APPLE CORER-WEDGER

The stainless steel corer-wedger that I prefer makes ten uniform wedge slices and removes the central one half inch cylinder of core. The one pictured here shows twelve wedges, but I prefer ten. It's great for any occasion where you want fresh apple sections. At fall festivals, we serve apple samples all day long cut with this device. It's perfect for cored apple wedges to serve with a dip, cheese, or just plain. Folks who sell sliced apples with hot caramel sauce find this to be the perfect tool. Preschool teachers and Mom's can use it to serve up platters of apple wedges for hungry tots. For an apple snack, some prefer to bite into a whole apple. My own preference is to serve myself ten neat little coreless apple wedges cut with one easy motion by this tool.

Set a whole apple on a cutting board and press the corer-wedger down from stem to blossom end. A ten-petal "flower" unfolds around the cylinder of core. Free the apple wedges from the base by lifting, leaving the corer-wedger resting on the board. For even faster wedging, you can first slice a good quarter-inch from the blossom end of the apple so it rests flat on the cutting board. The wedges will then fall free and not stay attached where the tool didn't cut completely through the peel at the base of the apple. You can also compensate for a slightly lopsided apple shape by adjusting the angle of the initial leveling cut so the core stands straight up on the cutting board.

Occasionally, an apple with a lopsided core will stop the blades when you try to slice it. When that happens, take a knife and patiently cut the apple off the slicer - don't try to force the slicer through the hard core. The core will win and the slicer will break. This is the only way you'll ever break the more expensive slicers (from Germany), while cheaper models will quickly break even in normal use.

Liz has opened my eyes to the versatility of this device in cooking. In many recipes where she's using just two or three apples, Liz starts by cutting the apples with the wedger-corer. If she wants no skin, she then peels each wedge with a paring knife. Finally, she slices the wedges either lengthwise for thin crescents or crosswise for large chunks as the recipe requires. Liz's method of hand-peeling the wedges is fine for a few apples but for large quantities of thick crescents for cobblers, compotes, etc., I recommend first peeling whole apples on the machine then cutting the peeled apples with the corer-wedger.

I always start applesauce with washed, unpeeled apples cut with the corer-wedger, cooking down the thick crescents in fresh cider, then running the softened pulp through a food mill.

CRESCENTS, CHUNKS, AND DICE

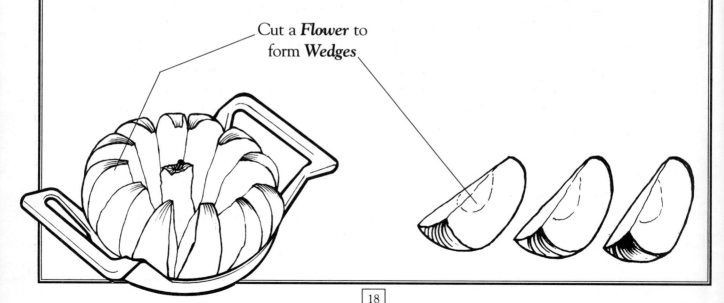

Cut a **Flower** to form **Wedges**

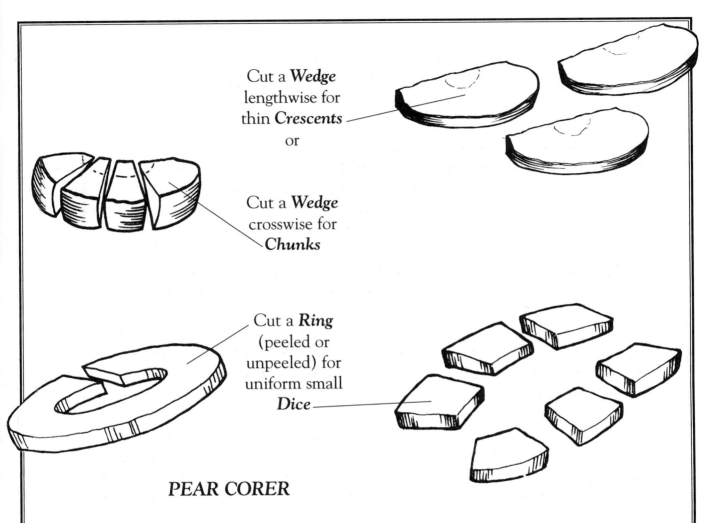

Cut a **Wedge** lengthwise for thin **Crescents**

or

Cut a **Wedge** crosswise for **Chunks**

Cut a **Ring** (peeled or unpeeled) for uniform small **Dice**

PEAR CORER

A fine tool for preparing apple quarters or halves for recipes or serving fresh is the pear corer. Elegantly simple, the design performs its function so perfectly that it's a joy to use. Its narrow cutting blade is curved into a rough teardrop shape and attached to a wooden handle. It's designed for pears but works just as well for apples.

Halve an apple by cutting from stem end to blossom end. Use the round side of the corer to remove the half circle center, then use the pointed end to cut a small wedge removing the strip of fiber running from stem to blossom end.

The advantage of this tool over a paring knife is that the central core section we want to remove from the apple is round while a paring knife is straight. Alternately, use a melon baller (or metal measuring spoon) to remove the semicircle and a sharp paring knife to cut the small vertical wedges. With the pear corer, it's all done in three smooth cuts - with no wasted motion changing tools. The pear corer is also handy for trimming out any bits of core missed by the apple peeling machine or corer/wedger when you're working with a large cored apple variety.

The pear corer works well with any size, shape, and texture of apple so can be used to core those lopsided or large apples that the machine can peel but can't core and slice. Then you can slice the peeled, cored apple halves any thickness you want.

Unpeeled, halved, cored apples are an elegant presentation for fresh apple snacks to be eaten out of hand or for poached apples. If you want to end up with peeled apples, peel them first either by hand or on the machine with the corer/slicer blade disengaged. Then cut the peeled apples in half and core them with the pear corer.

CORER WITH WOODEN PLUNGER

For baked apples, there is a stainless steel corer with a wooden plunger on the market that removes a wider core cylinder than other corers. To use the corer, set the whole apple on a cutting board and push the corer down the center. You may want to leave some core at the base or to cut all the way through. When you remove the corer, the apple core is stuck inside the metal tube and must be ejected with the wooden plunger. I have a love-hate relationship with this device because this part of the process is frustrating and tricky. Another caution with this device -- after some use, the wood collar at the top of the tube may come loose. When that happens, you can permanently re-attach it with "epoxy" glue. I only recommend this devise because I don't know of another one that does the job as well.

FOOD MILL

This device is invaluable for high-quality, low-labor, applesauce. It consists of a sturdy bottomless plastic bowl fitted with three interchangeable stainless steel screens for the bottom. A crank turned stainless steel paddle forces material through the screen for a smooth purée. The middle sized screen is perfect for smooth applesauce. Just wash the apples, there is no need to peel them and sacrifice the flavor and aroma that reside near the skin. You may also keep the cores, just quarter the apples and discard the stems, before putting them in the pot to cook down. I prefer to start with wedges from the corer-wedger; it's super fast and results in a less fibrous sauce.

After cooking the apples until they mush up, run the pulp through the food mill. The only trick I know of with this machine is to occasionally give the handle a few counterclockwise turns to clear the sieve before proceeding with clockwise turns.

Jill Vorbeck, Chapin, Illinois, 1994.

LEMON VERBENA AND
APPLE PEEL TEA

(1) Rinse a teapot with boiling water to warm it.
(2) Place the lemon verbena and apple peel in the teapot.
(3) Pour boiling water into the pot to fill it.
(4) Cover and allow to steep for 5 minutes before serving.

 INGREDIENTS

10-12 crumbled dried leaves of lemon verbena
peel from 1 apple (the more fragrant the apple, the more flavorful the tea)

MAKES ONE POT

HOT BUTTERED CIDER AND RUM

(1) Place the cider in a large enameled stock pot.
(2) Bring the cider to a simmer over medium heat.
(3) Add rum and butter and heat through until butter is just melted.
(4) Grate nutmeg over top of butter.
(5) Ladle cider into warm mugs and serve.

NOTE: *If you're planning a festive party or fall hayride, this is just the drink to warm chilled bones!*

INGREDIENTS

2 quarts of apple cider
1 cup of dark rum
3 tablespoons of butter
1/2 teaspoon of freshly grated nutmeg

SERVES 8

AUTUMN CIDER
AND CHAMPAGNE APERITIF

(1) Chill both the cider and the champagne.
(2) Fill the champagne glasses half full of cider.
(3) Top off the other half with the champagne.

NOTE: *A true taste of autumn, we toasted the beginning of fall in the cooking class with this light aperitif. This aperitif has the added benefit of stretching a few bottles of champagne to serve a crowd.*

 INGREDIENTS

1 gallon of good quality fresh cider
4 bottles of inexpensive champagne

SERVES 16

CHICKEN LIVER PÂTÉ
WITH APPLES

(1) Combine the currants and cognac. Bring to a boil, remove from heat and cool.

(2) Melt half of the butter in a heavy enameled skillet over medium heat.

(3) **Quick Trick**: Peel, core, and slice apple on "the machine." Cut the spiral into dice with a paring knife.

(4) Add the onion and 2/3 of the apple and sauté until the onion is transparent.

(5) Add the chicken livers and sauté until just pink. (Do not overcook or liver can become unpleasantly bitter.)

(6) Drain the cognac from the currants and add the cognac to the skillet with the livers.

(7) Stir in all of the spices and sauté for another minute, stirring constantly.

(8) Remove from the heat and cool slightly.

(9) In a small enameled skillet melt 2 tablespoons of the remaining butter.

(10) Sauté the remaining apple until it is just barely softened.

(11) Stir in the currants. Remove from the heat and cool.

(12) In a food processor fitted with the steel blade, purée the livers with the remaining butter.

(13) Scrape the pureed mixture into a bowl and with a spatula fold in the sautéed apple and currants. Mix completely.

(14) Add salt to taste.

(15) Pack the mixture into a pâté dish; chill.

(16) Garnish the dish with a sprig of apple mint or an edible autumn flower such as a chrysanthemum.

(17) Serve with lightly toasted slices of French loaves and apple wedges.

NOTE: The elegance and the mellow flavor of this appetizer pâté belie the simplicity of the ingredients. Even people who think they don't like liver-based pâtés will be seduced by the subtle underlying sweetness created by puréeing the apple with the liver. Sweet spices and currants are a surprise to the expected savory bite of most pâtés.

NOTE: If you have saved duck livers, by all means substitute them for the chicken livers. The unctuous combination of apples and duck liver is a perfect taste pairing.

INGREDIENTS

1/4 cup of dried currants
1/4 cup of Cognac or brandy
1/2 pound butter
1/2 medium sweet onion, diced
1 large aromatic apple, peeled and diced
1 pound chicken livers
1 teaspoon of salt
2 whole cloves
1/2 teaspoon of cinnamon
1/4 teaspoon of allspice
1/4 teaspoon of ground ginger
1/4 teaspoon of white pepper

SERVES 12 AS AN APPETIZER

APPLE TEMPURA RUMAKIS

(1) **Quick Trick:** Cut one apple with the corer-wedger, then cut each wedge crosswise into four chunks.

(2) Wrap a chicken liver around an apple cube.

(3) Surround both with a strip of bacon, and impale the bundle on a toothpick, being sure to secure both ends of the strip of bacon.

(4) Place the bacon-wrapped livers and apples on a cookie sheet.

(5) Mix together the flour and salt.

(6) Add the egg and enough water to make the batter the consistency of heavy whipping cream.

(7) Heat 4 inches of vegetable oil in a wok to 375° F.

(8) Using tongs, dip the rumaki, a few at a time, in the batter, turning them to coat all sides.

(9) Carefully lower them into the hot oil. Do not crowd the wok - about 4 rumaki at a time is enough.

(10) Turn the rumaki when they begin to brown and crisp. When the bacon has crisped, the rumaki are cooked through.

(11) Remove with a slotted spoon or Oriental strainer.

(12) Drain on paper towels.

(13) Serve warm.

NOTE: The rumaki here takes on a new character as cubes of Empire apple are substituted for the standard water chestnuts. Liz has further dressed up these classics by dipping them in a feather-light tempura batter before frying.

NOTE: The livers should just be pink. People who think they don't like liver often never had it any other way than over-cooked. The minute it becomes stiff and leathery, it turns unpleasantly bitter.

INGREDIENTS

24 whole chicken livers
24 1/2-inch chunks of firm-fleshed
  apples with peel
24 half strips of thick-sliced bacon
round wooden toothpicks for
  skewering
vegetable oil for deep frying

Tempura Batter

1/2 cup of all-purpose flour
1 teaspoon of salt
1 extra-large egg
water
vegetable oil for frying

SERVES 8

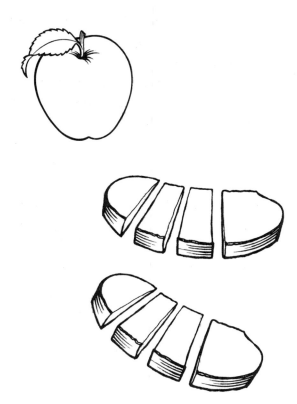

MARK'S LIVER
AND APPLE CANAPÉS

(1) Heat an enameled cast iron skillet over medium high heat.

(2) Add the clarified butter.

(3) Sauté the duck livers, turning once for about 2 minutes, or until they just begin to color and firm; but remain rare.

(4) Remove livers to a cutting board and reserve.

(5) *Quick Trick:* Use corer-wedger to section and core the apples. Peel each wedge, then halve it lengthwise with a paring knife to form two crescents.

(6) Add apple slices to skillet and sauté for about 2 minutes. (Apples should just warm through, but remain crisp.)

(7) Slice livers with a sharp knife, into thin slices, approximately the same size as the apple slices.

(8) Alternate liver and apple slices on the toasts, approximately two of each on each piece.

(9) Add the Madeira to the skillet, and with a spatula scrape any browned bits from the bottom of the pan.

(10) Allow the pan juices to boil and reduce until thickened. (About 3 tablespoons of sauce should remain.)

(11) Spoon a bit of the sauce over each canapé and serve immediately.

NOTE: In our "Everything but the Quack. . . " class, long-time resident wine expert Mark Drummond jumped in to demonstrate this canapé, which he and wife Shay prepare whenever they have a surfeit of duck livers. We made the toasts from one of Liz's French loaves, but Mark says toast points will serve equally well.

NOTE: To make clarified butter, melt 6 tablespoons of unsalted butter over medium heat. Cool. Gently pour off clear liquid. Stop pouring when white milky solids begin to appear.

INGREDIENTS

4 tablespoons of clarified butter
4 duck livers
2 tart apples, peeled and sliced
1/2 cup of Madeira
12 toasts made from slices of
    French loaves

MAKES 12

TAILGATE PEA SOUP
WITH APPLES

(1) Cut the meat from the ham hocks into 1/2-inch dice.

(2) In a large enameled Dutch oven, over medium heat, place the fatty pieces of the ham. If there is very little fat, add the bacon fat or butter.

(3) When the ham has rendered most of its fat, add the lean dice and bone; allow to brown, stirring frequently.

(4) Stir in the onion, celery, and carrots.

(5) Sauté, stirring frequently, until onion is translucent.

(6) Add garlic and stir for another minute.

(7) Stir in bay leaves, mint, crushed red pepper, and allspice berries.

(8) Sauté for one more minute, then add chicken stock.

(9) Bring stock to a boil scraping the bottom of the pan to incorporate any of the caramelized bits.

(10) Add the dried peas, reduce the heat and simmer for about 1 hour, or until the peas are soft.

(11) *Quick Trick:* Run the apples through "the machine," then cut the spiral with the corer-wedger to produce uniform small dice.

(12) Add the diced apple and stir.

(13) Simmer soup for another 15 minutes, or until apple has softened, but not disintegrated.

(14) Add sherry and simmer another 5 minutes to mellow flavor.

NOTE: *October, football, and apples! Brisk, bracing images of autumn leaves, chrysanthemum corsages, and tailgate picnics before the big game! Thermoses of hot soup are one of the most welcoming of all foods at a tailgate party, and pea soup is certainly high on everyone's list of favorites. In this hearty soup Liz has added diced apples to her full-flavored split-pea soup that she has been making since her years at the farm. Dig out the plaid wool lap robes, find a wide-mouthed thermos, and head for the stadium!*

NOTE: *Like any complex flavored soup, this one benefits from being made at least a day ahead and reheated.*

INGREDIENTS

2 pounds of meaty ham hocks, including bone

3-4 tablespoons of bacon fat or butter, if necessary

2 large yellow onions, peeled and diced

1 cup of diced celery, including leaves

2 large carrots, peeled and diced

3 large garlic cloves, peeled and minced

4 bay leaves

2 teaspoons of dried mint

1 teaspoon of crushed red pepper

12 whole allspice berries

3 quarts of strong chicken stock

1 pound of dried split peas

2 large crisp apples, cored, peeled, and diced

1/2 cup of dry sherry

SERVES 12

AUTUMN SQUASH
AND APPLE BISQUE

(1) Melt butter in a heavy-bottomed Dutch oven over medium heat.

(2) Add onions, ginger, and cinnamon.

(3) Sauté, stirring constantly, until onions are transparent.

(4) **Quick Trick:** Peel, core, and slice the apples with "the machine." Make about eight cuts through the spiral to dice.

(5) Add chicken stock, squash, and apples and bring to a boil.

(6) Simmer until squash and apples are soft.

(7) Cool mixture slightly.

(8) Purée in a blender, filling the container no more than 3/4 full.

(9) Add whipping cream, sherry, and season to taste with sea salt and cayenne pepper.

(10) Return to heat and warm through.

(11) Pass more sherry at the table, if desired.

NOTE: *Serve this rich, intriguingly flavored, soup in demitasse cups as a starter, or in larger bowls as a first course.*

🍎 INGREDIENTS

8 tablespoons of butter

2 large yellow onions, peeled and chopped

1 teaspoon of ginger

1 teaspoon of cinnamon

2 quarts of chicken stock

4 medium autumn squash (about 3 pounds total), such as acorn, butternut, or hubbard, peeled, seeded, and diced

5 firm-fleshed apples, cored, peeled, and diced

1 cup of heavy whipping cream

1/2 cup of dry sherry

sea salt and cayenne pepper to taste

SERVES 12 AS A FIRST COURSE

POTATO SOUP
WITH CHEDDAR CHEESE AND APPLE

(1) Melt the butter in a heavy enameled Dutch oven over medium heat.

(2) Add the onions and bay leaves and sauté, stirring constantly, until the onions are transparent.

(3) **Quick Trick:** Peel, core, and slice the apples on "the machine." Make about eight cuts through the spiral to dice.

(4) Add the chicken stock, apples, and potatoes, and bring to a boil.

(5) Reduce heat and simmer until apples and potatoes are soft.

(6) Cool the mixture slightly.

(7) Remove bay leaves.

(8) Purée in a blender with the diced cheese, taking care to fill the blender only 3/4 full each time.

(9) Stir cream and sherry into the soup.

(10) Season to taste with sea salt and cayenne pepper.

(11) Return soup to low heat and heat through, stirring frequently. Do not allow soup to boil or cheese will curdle!

INGREDIENTS

8 tablespoons of butter

2 medium yellow onions, peeled and chopped

4 bay leaves

2 quarts of chicken stock

4 firm-fleshed apples, peeled, cored, and diced

5 medium Idaho Russet potatoes, peeled and diced

8 ounces of extra sharp cheddar cheese, diced

1 cup of heavy whipping cream

1/2 cup of dry sherry

sea salt and cayenne pepper, to taste

NOTE: *This soup marries two perennial favorites in an unexpected way. A fabulous beginning for an autumn dinner party or a wonderful main course for a soup and salad luncheon!*

SERVES 12

BLUE CHEESE OMELET
WITH APPLES AND WALNUTS

Preheat oven to 300° F.

(1) Toast the walnuts for 15 minutes; set aside.
(2) ***Quick Trick:*** Peel, core, and slice the apple with the peeler, corer, and slicer. Cut one diameter through the spiral to form thin, peeled rainbows.
(3) In a heavy enameled skillet, over medium heat, sauté the apple slices in 2 tablespoons of butter until they begin to brown.
(4) Remove from heat and reserve.
(5) In a bowl, whisk together the eggs, water, salt, pepper, and cinnamon.
(6) Melt the remaining 2 tablespoons of butter in an omelet pan over medium-high heat. When the butter begins to foam, tilt the pan to coat the entire surface.
(7) Quickly pour in the egg mixture, and with a fork lift the edges of the omelet the moment that it starts to set, tilting the pan to allow the liquid egg to run under the omelet. Work all the way around the pan, tilting in all directions to insure an even thickness.
(8) When only a little liquid egg remains on the surface of the omelet, distribute the cheese in a line down the center of the pan.
(9) Top the cheese with the nuts and apples.
(10) Using the fork, flip one half of the omelet over the filling and slide the omelet out of the pan onto a warm plate.
(11) Allow the omelet to rest for about 2 minutes for the cheese to melt and the flavors to blend.

NOTE: Apples and eggs? Why not? The subtle sweetness of the sautéed apples blends beautifully with the crunch of the nuts and mellowness of the cheese, for an intriguing dish that becomes a very "upscale" quick brunch or lunch.

NOTE: To make an Apple Pecan Camembert Omelet substitute Camembert cheese for blue cheese and pecans for walnuts.

 INGREDIENTS

2 tablespoons of chopped walnuts
1 small sweet apple, cored, peeled and sliced
4 tablespoons of butter, divided
3 extra-large eggs
1 tablespoon of water
1 teaspoon of salt
2 or 3 grinds of fresh pepper (to taste)
2 ounces of good quality blue cheese

NOTE: Although it's easy enough to peel and slice a single apple "by hand," if you have a "machine," you might as well flaunt it!

SERVES 2

APPLE BREAKFAST SAUSAGE

(1) Quarter and core the apple, then grate in the food processor or on a hand grater.
(2) Combine all the pork, apple, onion, thyme, mace, salt, pepper, and egg in a plastic or ceramic bowl.
(3) Mix thoroughly with your hands.
(4) Test your sausage by sautéing a spoonful in a tablespoon of butter over medium heat.
(5) Taste and adjust seasonings.
(6) Form the sausage mixture into 4 patties. (This is a very wet mixture, but don't be alarmed.)
(7) In a heavy enameled skillet, over medium heat, melt 4 tablespoons of butter.
(8) Add the sausages and press down gently with the back of a spatula.
(9) Sauté for 4 minutes or until the bottom of the sausage begins to brown.
(10) Turn the sausages and sauté for 4 more minutes on the other side.
(11) Turn the sausages again. Check one patty to see that the interior is cooked through.

INGREDIENTS

1 pound of freshly ground pork
1 medium, tart apple, cored and grated, but not peeled
1 small yellow onion, peeled and chopped fine
1 tablespoon of fresh thyme, minced (1 teaspoon dried)
1/2 teaspoon of ground mace
1 teaspoon of sea salt
1/2 teaspoon of freshly ground pepper, or to taste
1 extra-large egg
5 tablespoons of butter

NOTE: If dietary restrictions preclude pork, this sausage can be equally delicious made with freshly ground turkey, chicken, or venison.

SERVES 4

EARLY TRANSPARENT
APPLESAUCE

(1) **Quick Tip:** Cut the apples into wedges with the corer-wedger.

(2) Place the apples in a heavy bottomed enameled Dutch oven large enough to hold them.

(3) Add the water.

(4) Place over medium low heat, and stir constantly. The apples will begin to give up their moisture. Cook until soft.

(5) Place apples in a food mill and process into a large bowl. Discard cores and peels left in the food mill.

(6) Season the applesauce with sugar to taste.

(7) Add optional cinnamon and lemon juice, if desired.

INGREDIENTS

6 pounds of Early Transparent apples (or other sauce apple), quartered and sectioned, but not peeled

1/2 cup of water

3/4-1 cup of sugar, or to taste

1 teaspoon of ground cinnamon (optional)

1 tablespoon of lemon juice (optional)

NOTE: Since she first began gardening for Liz, Barb Harrison has extolled the virtues of Early Transparent Apples for applesauce. In Liz's "Summer Produce" cooking class, Barb began the recipe, then Alice Laws offered her amendments. They both used the same techniques, but with different seasonings.

SERVES 8

SOUR CREAM AND MUSTARD
APPLESAUCE

(1) **Quick Trick:** Cut the apples into wedges with the corer-wedger.
(2) Place the apple sections in an enameled pan.
(3) Add just enough water to barely cover.
(4) Bring to a boil over medium high heat.
(5) Reduce heat and simmer until water is almost evaporated and apples are soft.
(6) Place contents of sauce pan in a food mill and process into a non-reactive bowl.
(7) Whisk in sour cream and mustard.
(8) Serve with roast beef, game, or poultry.

 INGREDIENTS

3 large fragrant apples, cored and sectioned, but not peeled
1 cup of sour cream
1/2 cup of sweet, grainy mustard

MAKES ABOUT 2 CUPS

SMOKED BRATWURST
WITH SAUERKRAUT AND APPLES

Preheat oven to 375° F.

(1) Parboil the bratwurst for 10 minutes. Drain and set aside.
(2) In a heavy enameled skillet, melt the bacon fat over medium heat.
(3) Sauté the onion until transparent.
(4) *Quick Trick:* Core and wedge the apples with the corer-wedger; cut each wedge into fourths with a paring knife.
(5) Add the apples, potatoes, bay leaves, caraway seeds, and thyme.
(6) Stir until apples begin to soften.
(7) Add the sauerkraut and mix thoroughly.
(8) Stir in the chicken stock.
(9) Lightly oil an oval enameled or porcelain au gratin dish. Cover bottom with a layer of the sauerkraut mixture.
(10) Lay the bratwursts over the sauerkraut.
(11) Cover the bratwursts with the remaining sauerkraut mixture.
(12) Pour the cream over the entire dish.
(13) Bake for 35 minutes, or until the liquid forms thick bubbles around the edge of the dish and the sauerkraut begins to brown slightly on top.

INGREDIENTS

6 smoked bratwurst, parboiled and drained
6 tablespoons of bacon fat
1 large yellow onion, peeled and diced
3 medium firm red apples, cored and diced, but not peeled
2 medium red potatoes, peeled and diced
3 bay leaves
1 tablespoon of caraway seeds
2 teaspoons of dried thyme (2 tablespoons fresh)
1 pound quality sauerkraut rinsed and squeezed dry
1 teaspoon of freshly grated pepper
1/2 cup of very strong chicken stock
1/2 cup of heavy whipping cream

SERVES 6

ROAST CHICKEN
WITH LOVEAGE

Preheat oven to 450° F.

(1) Wash and dry chicken, rinsing cavity thoroughly.

(2) Salt the cavity.

(3) **Quick Trick:** Cut the apples into quarters, then core with the pear-corer.

(4) Place all but one of the apple quarters in the cavity of the chicken.

(5) Pack the loveage and sorrel into the cavity.

(6) Place the remaining apple quarter, skin side out, across the opening of the cavity.

(7) Using kitchen twine, secure the wings to the body, and tie the legs together.

(8) Salt the skin of the chicken and place the bird, breast side up, on a rack in a roasting pan.

(9) Place the chicken in the oven and roast undisturbed for 30 minutes.

(10) Reduce oven to 325° F.

(11) Pour 1/2 cup of the cider over the chicken. With a bulb baster, pull up the cider and pan juices and thoroughly baste the chicken.

(12) Continue to roast for approximately 30 minutes, basting every 10-15 minutes, adding the remaining cider as that in the roasting pan evaporates. The bird is done when it is golden and the juice runs clear when the thigh is pricked.

(13) Allow the chicken to roast, covered with foil, on a carving board for at least 15 minutes before slicing.

(14) Serve with some of the pan juices on each serving.

NOTE: Since Liz began teaching the cooking classes, she has become privy to some marvelous sources for supplies. Through her students she has met suppliers of mushrooms, fruits, produce, and game. One of her most treasured contacts is for free-range chickens. Anyone who grew up on a farm remembers with longing the taste of that farmyard chicken on the Sunday table. The giant roaster Liz used in this recipe was produced by one her students with the promise of anonymity! Lacking such a secret source, special order from your butcher for the largest roasting hen available.

 INGREDIENTS

1 large, 6-7 pound roasting chicken (free-range, if possible)
salt
2 firm red apples, quartered and cored
1 bunch of loveage (substitute celery tops and leaves if loveage is unavailable)
8-10 leaves of sorrel
sea salt
1 1/2 cups of cider

SERVES 6

ACORN SQUASH
STUFFED WITH LAMB AND CURRY

Preheat oven to 400° F.

(1) Cut the acorn squash in half from the stem to the tip and scrape out the seeds; set aside.
(2) In a heavy enameled skillet, over medium heat, melt the butter.
(3) Sauté the onion for 2-3 minutes.
(4) ***Quick Trick:*** Core and slice the apple on the peeler/corer/slicer machine with the peeling arm wedged out of action. Slice the spiral to form small, uniform dice.
(5) Add the apple, garlic, and curry powder.
(6) Sauté, stirring with a flat wooden spatula, for about 3 more minutes, or until apple is beginning to soften and curry has become quite fragrant.

(7) Add lamb and mix thoroughly, breaking up any chunks.
(8) Brown lamb and stir in cumin, cayenne, and salt.
(9) Add cream and allow to boil and reduce until thick.
(10) Pack as much of the lamb mixture as possible into the hollowed out squash halves.
(11) Place the squash in a baking dish just large enough to hold them upright. (A square Pyrex cake pan is ideal.)
(12) Pour 1 inch of boiling water in the dish and cover tightly with foil.
(13) Bake in the oven for 1 hour, or until the flesh of the squash is tender when pierced with a fork.

INGREDIENTS

1 large acorn squash (about 1 pound)
4 tablespoons of butter
1/2 medium yellow onion, peeled and diced
1 large tart apple, cored and diced
2 large garlic cloves, minced
2 teaspoons of good quality curry powder
1 pound ground lamb
1 teaspoon of cumin seed
1/2 teaspoon of cayenne pepper
1 teaspoon of salt, or to taste
1/2 cup of heavy whipping cream

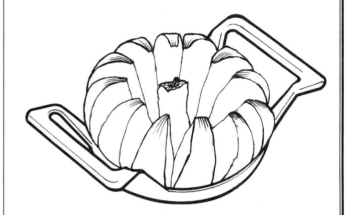

GARLIC

SERVES 2

CROWN ROAST OF PORK
WITH APPLE SAUSAGE DRESSING

Preheat oven to 450° F.

(1) Place crown roast on a rack in a roasting pan.

(2) Salt and pepper inside and out; set aside.

(3) In a large, heavy enameled cast iron skillet, sauté the sausage and onion, breaking up any lumps, until it has rendered its fat and changed color.

(4) ***Quick Trick:*** Core and slice the apple on the peeler/corer/slicer machine with the peeling arm wedged out of action. Slice the spirals to form small, uniform dice.

(5) Stir in diced apples and thyme and continue to cook for five more minutes.

(6) Drain sausage mixture through a colander to remove accumulated fat and liquid.

(7) Return sausage to skillet and season to taste with sea salt and pepper.

(8) Mix in eggs.

(9) Pack as much of the sausage mixture as possible into the top cavity of the crown roast. (see note)

(10) Place in the oven and roast for 1/2 hour.

(11) Reduce oven temperature to 400° F. and roast until temperature on an instant-read thermometer inserted into the base of the roast registers 140° F. (If pork that is beyond "pink" is desired, roast until temperature registers 150° F.)

(12) Remove roast from oven and allow to rest for about 30 minutes before carving. The internal temperature of the meat will continue to rise another 5 to 10 degrees.

(13) Remove roast to a carving board.

(14) To serve, slice down between each rib. Allow one rib and some of the stuffing for each serving.

INGREDIENTS

1 12-rib crown roast of pork
sea salt and freshly ground pepper
3 pounds mild pork sausage
2 medium yellow onions peeled
   and finely chopped
3 large, tart apples, cored and diced
   but not peeled
3 tablespoons of finely minced
   fresh thyme (1 tablespoon dried)
3 extra-large eggs, slightly beaten

NOTE: *Any apple sausage dressing
that does not fit into the cavity of
the crown roast may be baked sepa-
rately in another pan. Bake at 350°
F. for about 30 minutes, or until
the top is just browned.*

SERVES 12

BOURBON PAN GRAVY

(1) Remove the rack from the roasting
   pan and place the pan on the front
   burner of your stove over medium
   heat.
(2) Using a flat wooden spatula, scrape
   up any browned bits from the bottom of the roasting pan.
(3) Add the Bourbon Whiskey to the
   pan.
(4) Allow to boil while continuing to
   scrape and stir.
(5) When gravy has thickened to the
   color and consistency of chocolate
   syrup, pour through a sieve into a
   gravy boat.
(6) Salt to taste.
(7) Pass with the crown roast.

 INGREDIENTS

1/2 cup of Bourbon Whiskey

PORK CHOPS
WITH APPLES AND BACON

(1) In a heavy-bottomed enameled skillet, over medium heat, sauté the bacon until fat is rendered and bacon is crisp.

(2) Remove to a paper towel and reserve.

(3) **Quick Trick:** Core and wedge the apples with the corer-wedger.

(4) In the bacon fat, sauté the apples over medium heat until they are soft, but not mushy. The cut edges should brown and caramelize.

(5) Remove the apples with a slotted spoon and keep warm.

(6) In a brown paper bag place the flour, salt and pepper. Shake to mix thoroughly.

(7) Shake the pork chops in the seasoned flour.

(8) Fry the pork chops in the remaining fat, over medium high heat until they are browned, turning once.

(9) Serve the chops on warmed plates, covered with the apples and 4 pieces of bacon per chop.

INGREDIENTS

12 strips of thick-sliced slab bacon, halved
6 small sweet apples
6 thin-sliced, bone-on rib pork chops
1 cup of all-purpose flour
2 teaspoons of salt
1 teaspoon of pepper

NOTE: A farm childhood puts you close to the land and very much attuned to the changing seasons. Apples and pork are a combination that comes as automatically as the first frost and falling leaves. Liz's mother always fried the apples and pork chops in bacon fat - a taste match that's hard to beat. If dietary restrictions preclude the bacon fat, you may substitute the low cholesterol oils, but at a marked sacrifice to authentic flavor.

SERVES 6

CIDER BARBECUE SAUCE

(1) Put the cider in a large enameled sauce pan.

(2) Bring it to a boil, watching carefully so as not to let it boil over.

(3) Reduce heat and simmer until cider is reduced by half.

(4) Add the cider vinegar, butter, soy sauce, brown sugar, onion, garlic, cloves, cinnamon stick, bay leaves Worcestershire Sauce, hot pepper sauce, mustard, and catsup.

(5) Stir until sugar is completely dissolved and mustard is thoroughly incorporated.

(6) Simmer the sauce, stirring from time to time, until the sauce has reduced to about 2 cups. (This might take up to 5 or 6 hours.) It should coat the back of a wooden spoon. Do not be tempted to raise the heat to accelerate the reduction. You do not want to scorch the sauce.

NOTE: This sauce keeps well when covered and refrigerated.

INGREDIENTS

2 1/2 quarts of apple cider
1/2 cup of cider vinegar
3 tablespoons of butter
1/4 cup of soy sauce
1/2 cup of brown sugar
1 small yellow onion, minced
4 large garlic cloves, minced
3 whole cloves
2-inch piece of cinnamon stick
3 bay leaves
1 tablespoon of Worcestershire Sauce
1/2 teaspoon of Tabasco or other hot pepper sauce (more to taste)
2 tablespoons of top quality grainy mustard
8 ounces of tomato catsup

MAKES 2 CUPS

BRAISED HAM
IN AN APPLE WINE CREAM SAUCE

(1) Place ham in a non-reactive pot (enameled cast iron) large enough to hold it and cover with cold water.

(2) Add onions, carrots, celery, cloves, peppercorns, all-spice, bay leaves, thyme, and apple wine.

(3) Simmer for 2-3 hours, or until ham is tender but not falling off the bone.

(4) Remove ham to a carving board.

(5) Boil cooking liquid until it is reduced to about 3 cups.

(6) Strain to remove vegetables and spices.

(7) Return cooking liquid to a small non-reactive pan.

(8) Taste for salt. If juices are terribly salty, discard half of them and replace with more wine or plain water.

(9) Boil liquid until reduced to about 2 cups.

(10) Add whipping cream.

(11) Continue to boil until reduced again to about 2 cups.

(12) **Quick Trick:** Core and section the apples with the corer-wedger, but leave their skins intact.

(13) Melt the butter in a large enameled skillet over medium-high heat.

(14) Add the apple slices and sauté, stirring with a wooden spatula, until softened, but still holding their shape.

(15) Stir sautéed apple slices into the reduced apple/cream sauce and pour into a sauce boat to be served with the sliced ham.

NOTE: Most Colonial villages that trade on tourism can produce a smoke house with some very respectable products, and a winery with some very "interesting" products. (Iowa's Amana Colonies are no exception. Their hams, bacon, and brats are excellent products. An Amana Ham is the basis for this dish, though any quality smoked ham could be substituted.) The wines distilled from regional fruits, which are sampled in tasting cellars, are not to the normal wine drinker's taste. If communion grape juice is your idea of wine, perhaps you can appreciate them, but for the average tourist they present a novelty and a souvenir. In cooking, however, these extraordinarily fruity wines can have their place.

INGREDIENTS

1 large (12 pound) bone-in ham
3 large yellow onions, peeled and chunked
4 carrots peeled and chunked
4 ribs of celery cut into 2-inch pieces
4 cloves
12 whole black peppercorns
12 whole allspice berries
4 bay leaves
2 teaspoons of dried thyme (2 tablespoons fresh)
1 fifth Apple Wine
salt, if necessary
2 cups of heavy whipping cream

2 firm, fragrant cooking apples
4 tablespoons of butter

SERVES 30 AS PART OF A BUFFET

OVEN-BARBECUED
PORK TENDERLOINS

Preheat oven to 400° F.

(1) **Quick Trick:** Run the apples through "the machine" with the peeling blade disengaged.
(2) Place one half of the onions and apples on the bottom of a small heavy roasting pan. (An enameled cast iron pan with a non-stick surface is ideal for this.)
(3) Rub salt and pepper into the surface of the pork tenders and lay them on top of the apples and onions, tucking the small end under, in order to equalize the width of the tenderloin.
(4) Cover the tenders with the other half of the apples and onions.
(5) Wrap foil over the top of the roasting pan and crimp the edges to cover tightly.

(6) Place the pan on the center shelf of the preheated oven and roast undisturbed for 45 minutes.
(7) Remove the pan from the oven and carefully remove the foil. Steam will rush out, so lift a corner away from you first.
(8) Push the apples and onions off the tenderloins and brush the tenders thoroughly with the Cider Barbecue Sauce.
(9) Return the pan to the oven for 10 minutes.
(10) Repeat the basting process 3 more times at 10 minute intervals.
(11) Place the tenders on a cutting board and allow to rest for at least 10 minutes.
(12) Slice on the diagonal to serve.
(13) To serve place several slices of meat and some of the apples and onions on each plate.

NOTE: *For country style ribs, substitute 2 meaty country-style ribs per person for the pork tenderloins. Follow the same procedure as for the tenderloins, placing the ribs, bone-side down, about 1 inch apart on the apples and onions. Allow 1 hour of roasting time before removing the foil. Proceed with the basting as for the tenderloins.*

INGREDIENTS

2 whole true pork tenderloins (about 1/2 to 1 pound each)

3 large, firm, sweet apples, cored but not peeled, and sliced

3 medium yellow onions, peeled and sliced

sea salt and freshly ground pepper, to taste

Cider Barbecue Sauce (see page 47)

SERVES 6

AUTUMN ROAST DUCKLING
WITH APPLES

(1) Soak the bottom and lid of a Romertoph or other unglazed clay roasting pot in warm water for fifteen minutes.

(2) Remove the neck and giblets from the cavity of the duck. Reserve the liver for pâté or another purpose.

(3) Place the neck and giblets in the bottom of the clay pot to serve as a base for the duck.

(4) Wash the duck and pat dry with paper towels.

(5) Salt and pepper the duck inside and out.

(6) Place the duck in the clay pot, breast side up, and cover. Place roasting pot on the center shelf of a cold oven.

(7) Immediately turn the oven temperature to 450° F.

(8) Roast the duck, undisturbed for 1 hour.

(9) **Quick Trick:** Use the corer-wedger to core and slice the apples.

(10) Remove the lid and place the apple slices around the duck.

(11) Pour the Calvados over the duck and with a bulb baster pull the duck drippings and Calvados up from the bottom of the pot and baste duck and apples several times.

(12) Return the pot, uncovered, to the oven and roast for another 30 minutes, basting every 10 minutes, or until duck skin is brown and apples are soft, but not mushy.

(13) Remove duck to a carving board and allow to rest for 15 minutes.

(14) To serve, carve some of the breast meat and thigh meat for each plate and accompany with the apples.

NOTE: Long a European favorite, duck is much underutilized on American menus. One of Liz's favorite meats (she swears she would request it on her "last meal" menu!), she cooks it far more frequently than most other poultry. The unglazed clay roasting pot makes draining the fat from the meat effortless. The savory bird stays moist while the excess fat is rendered.

NOTE: Be sure to save the duck fat. Sweet potatoes, turnips, or potatoes sautéed in the fat are the perfect accompaniment to this duck!

INGREDIENTS

1 5-pound Long Island Duckling, thawed
2 teaspoons of sea salt
1 teaspoon of freshly ground pepper
3 apples, cored and sliced, but not peeled
1/2 cup of Calvados or Applejack

SERVES 4

CIDER-MARINATED
VENISON ROAST

Preheat oven to 425° F.

(1) Place the venison roast in a deep, non-reactive (enameled cast iron) bowl.

(2) Pour in enough cider to completely cover the meat to determine the correct amount for the marinade.

(3) Pour the cider off into an enameled Dutch oven large enough to hold it.

(4) Add all the remaining ingredients.

(5) Bring the marinade to a boil over medium high heat.

(6) Reduce heat and simmer for 10 minutes.

(7) Pour the hot marinade over the venison and allow to cool to room temperature.

(8) Refrigerate meat and marinade for 24 hours. Turn the meat once or twice during this time.

(9) Remove meat from the marinade and pat dry.

(10) Put marinade in an enameled Dutch oven and bring to a boil.

(11) Reduce heat and simmer for 15 minutes then remove from heat.

(12) Meanwhile, place meat on a rack in a roasting pan and lightly salt and pepper the outside of the roast.

(13) Place roast on center shelf of preheated oven. Roast for 30 minutes.

(14) Reduce oven temperature to 350° F. and remove pan from oven.

(15) With a bulb baster, baste roast with some of the liquid from the heated marinade.

(16) Return roast to oven. Continue to baste every 10 minutes until internal temperature of venison reaches 140° F. when an instant-read thermometer is inserted into the meat.

(17) Remove roast from oven and baste with remaining pan juices.

(18) Allow roast to rest for about 20 minutes before carving.

(19) Slice thin slices from the roast, carving parallel to the bone. Serve with Sour Cream and Mustard Applesauce.

INGREDIENTS

1 4-pound venison shoulder roast
cider to cover
1/2 cup of cider vinegar
5 bay leaves
1 4-inch stick of cinnamon
5 whole cloves
1 teaspoon of whole allspice
1 tablespoon of whole peppercorns
1 tablespoon of dried thyme
2-inch piece of fresh ginger,
　unpeeled, sliced
2 tablespoons of salt
1 firm tart red apple, cored but not
　peeled, cut into wedges
1 medium yellow onion, peeled and
　chunked
1/2 cup of chopped celery tops and
　leaves
1 medium carrot, peeled and chunked
3 large garlic cloves, peeled and
　sliced
Sour Cream and Mustard Applesauce
　(see page 38)

SERVES 6

CHURCH SUPPER BAKED BEANS
WITH BACON LATTICE TOPPING

(1) Cover the beans with cold water in a cast iron enameled Dutch oven large enough to hold them.

(2) Run your fingers through the beans and discard any shriveled beans or pebbles. (Do not salt the water, as this will toughen the beans.)

(3) Bring the water to a boil over medium high heat.

(4) Allow to boil for 2 or 3 minutes.

(5) Remove beans from heat and allow to rest for 2-3 hours. Drain beans and discard liquid.

(6) Place the beans back in the Dutch oven and cover with fresh cold water, and once again bring to a boil.

(7) Reduce heat to medium and simmer until beans are tender to the bite (about 1 hour).

(8) Add the salt to the cooking water once the beans are tender.

Preheat oven to 350° F.

(9) Drain the beans, reserving the cooking liquid.

(10) Place the beans in a 9x12-inch cast iron or glass baking dish.

(11) ***Quick Trick:*** Wedge the peeler blade out of action, then core and slice the apples on "the machine." Slice the spiral to form uniform dice.

(12) Add the onion, apples, and bacon and mix thoroughly.

(13) In a 2-cup glass measuring cup, combine the brown sugar, molasses, cider vinegar, mustard, red pepper, ginger, allspice, and enough of the reserved bean liquid to equal 2 cups.

(14) Pour this mixture over the beans and mix again.

(15) Cover the pan with aluminum foil and crimp the edges to seal.

(16) Place on the center shelf of the preheated oven and bake undisturbed for 1 hour.

(17) Remove beans from oven and reduce oven temperature to 300° F. Lift the foil from a corner away from you, as the steam will rush out.

(18) Check the level of the liquid, adding more bean cooking liquid if a great

deal has evaporated.

(19) Recover the beans with the foil and return to the oven for 1 hour longer.

(20) When the beans have baked for another hour, remove the pan from the oven and remove the foil.

(21) Taste a bean for tenderness and return the pan to the oven for a while longer, if necessary.

(22) Meanwhile, on a 12x14-inch baking sheet with sides, weave the bacon strips like a children's paper place mat, to form a rectangle slightly larger than the pan containing the beans. Leave approximately 1 1/2 inches between the woven rows of bacon, as you want the beans to show through the lattice in the final presentation.

(23) Place bacon lattice in oven; cook until crisp. Pour off rendered fat.

(24) When the beans are tender, place the bacon lattice on top of the beans; return the beans to the oven to warm bacon through.

INGREDIENTS

1 pound of Great Northern beans
water to cover
2 teaspoons of salt
1 large yellow onion peeled and diced
2 large firm apples, cored and diced but not peeled
1/4 pound of thick slab bacon, diced
1/2 cup of dark brown sugar, firmly packed
1/4 cup of dark molasses
1/4 cup of cider vinegar
2 teaspoons of dry mustard
1/2 teaspoon of crushed red pepper
1 teaspoon of ground ginger
1 teaspoon of ground allspice
reserved liquid from cooking beans

1/2 pound of thick slab bacon

SERVES 12

BRAISED RED CABBAGE
AND CHESTNUTS

(1) Melt the butter in the bottom of a large cast iron enameled pan over medium heat.

(2) Add onions and sauté until they are transparent.

(3) *Quick Trick:* Peel, core, and slice the apples on "the machine." Cut the rings into small, uniform dice with a paring knife.

(4) Stir in cabbage, apples, thyme, and bay leaves into onion mixture.

(5) Cook, stirring constantly, until cabbage begins to wilt.

(6) Stir in the wine and chestnuts.

(7) Allow mixture to come to a boil then turn heat to medium low, cover pan, and simmer for about 1/2 hour.

(8) If a good deal of liquid remains, turn up heat and reduce.

(9) Season to taste with sea salt and pepper.

INGREDIENTS

1 large head of red cabbage, cored and shredded (set aside)

2 cups of cooked whole chestnuts, cooled and reserved

3 large, yellow onions, peeled and sliced

2 large cooking apples, peeled and diced

1 tablespoon of fresh thyme, minced (1 teaspoon dried)

4 bay leaves

2 cups of dry, red wine

sea salt and freshly ground pepper to taste

NOTE: This hearty winter vegetable dish is a perfect accompaniment to creamy cold-weather stews, pork, or game dishes. Dried, peeled chestnuts are available in Oriental markets, and need only a brief simmering to reconstitute.

SERVES 8

GRATIN OF APPLES
SWEET POTATOES AND ONIONS

Preheat oven to 350° F.

(1) Lightly spray a baking dish (a heavy, enameled cast iron dish with a non-stick surface is ideal) with non-stick coating spray.

(2) **Quick Trick:** Peel, core, and slice the apples on "the machine." Cut one radius through the spiral to form rings.

(3) Layer the apples, onions, and sweet potatoes in the dish, alternating layers until all of the slices are used.

(4) In a bowl, whisk together the eggs, cream, sea salt, nutmeg, and pepper.

(5) Pour the mixture over the apples, sweet potatoes, and onions.

(6) Dot the top of the dish with the 4 tablespoons of butter.

(7) Bake until puffed and golden, about 45 minutes.

🍎 INGREDIENTS

non-stick coating spray
6 firm-fleshed, tart apples cored, peeled, and sliced
2 medium yellow onions, peeled and sliced
5 medium sweet potatoes, peeled and sliced
5 extra-large eggs
1 cup of heavy whipping cream
sea salt, freshly grated nutmeg, and pepper to taste
4 tablespoons of butter, cut into bits

NOTE: *This ultimately fall-flavored dish is a natural accompaniment to any pork roast, game, or poultry. Sick of the usual sweet potatoes and marshmallows at Thanksgiving? Try substituting this gratin as a savory alternative!*

SERVES 8

GINGERED
CARROTS AND APPLES

(1) Peel carrots and grate through the shredding blade of a food processor or shred by hand using a grater.

(2) Place carrots in a sauce pan, cover with water and bring to a boil.

(3) Drain, pushing any excess water from the carrots.

(4) Shred the apple wedges in the food processor or by hand using a grater.

(5) Melt the butter in the sauce pan.

(6) Add the ginger and sauté, stirring constantly

(7) When ginger is fragrant, but not browned, add the apples and cook for 2 minutes, stirring constantly.

(8) Add the drained carrots and stir until warmed through.

(9) Season to taste with salt and pepper.

 INGREDIENTS

4 large carrots
2 firm, red skinned apples, cored and sectioned, but not peeled
1-inch piece of fresh ginger, peeled and grated
6 tablespoons of butter
sea salt and pepper to taste

SERVES 6

SCALLOPED CELERY
WITH APPLES AND ONIONS

Preheat oven to 350° F.

(1) In a heavy enameled skillet, over medium heat, melt 6 tablespoons of butter.

(2) Add onion, celery, bay leaves, and tarragon.

(3) Sauté, stirring frequently with a wooden spatula, until celery begins to soften and onion becomes translucent.

(4) Add apples and sauté another 5 minutes. Remove skillet from heat.

(5) Lightly spray an oval 8x11-inch enameled or earthenware au gratin dish with non-stick coating spray.

(6) With a slotted spoon, evenly distribute vegetable and apple mixture in dish.

(7) Whisk together eggs, cream, salt, pepper, and nutmeg. Pour over vegetables and apples.

(8) In a small, heavy skillet melt the remaining 2 tablespoons of butter over medium heat.

(9) Add the bread crumbs and sauté stirring constantly until they are toasted.

(10) Top the apple and vegetable mixture with the crumbs.

(11) Place the au gratin dish on the center rack and bake for 25 minutes.

INGREDIENTS

8 tablespoons of butter, divided
1 medium yellow onion, peeled and thinly sliced
3 cups of thinly sliced celery
3 bay leaves
1 tablespoon of minced fresh tarragon (or 1 teaspoon dried)
3 medium firm, sweet apples, cored, peeled, and sliced
non-stick coating spray
2 extra-large eggs
1 cup of heavy whipping cream
2 teaspoons of salt
good grating of white pepper (to taste)
1/2 teaspoon of freshly ground nutmeg
1 cup of fresh bread crumbs

SERVES 6

COLESLAW
WITH CHEDDAR CHEESE AND APPLES

(1) Combine cabbage, cheddar, apple, and onion in a bowl large enough to contain them.

(2) Using your hands, toss thoroughly, breaking up any clumps of the cheese.

(3) In a separate bowl, whisk together the mayonnaise, sour cream, ginger, cinnamon, mustard, salt, and cayenne pepper.

(4) Taste and adjust the seasonings to your taste.

(5) Stir the dressing into the slaw mixture and using your hands toss to thoroughly coat the slaw.

(6) Taste again for seasoning, adding more spices as necessary.

(7) Chill for at least 3 hours or preferably over-night in order for flavors to marry.

NOTE: *A beautiful presentation for an autumn buffet, this colorful slaw can be easily doubled or tripled to feed a crowd.*

INGREDIENTS

1 large head of green cabbage, finely shredded

4 cups of shredded sharp cheddar cheese

4 large red-skinned apples, cored and shredded, but not peeled

1 large yellow onion, shredded

1 1/2 cups of mayonnaise

1 1/2 cups of sour cream

2 teaspoons of ground ginger

1 teaspoon of ground cinnamon

1 teaspoon of dry mustard

sea salt and cayenne pepper, to taste

NOTE: *Liz garnishes the top of this slaw with a ring of shredded cheddar and a parsley bouquet surrounded by unpeeled apple wedges to form a "flower" in the center of the bowl.*

SERVES 12

BABY GARDEN GREEN SALAD

(1) Slice apples with corer-wedger, then cut each wedge into four pieces.
(2) In a large bowl, gently toss together the greens, onion, cheese, and apples.
(3) Dress the salad to taste with the fruit vinegar, hazelnut oil, sea salt, and pepper.

NOTE: *This salad turned out to be one of the unrivaled hits of our apple cooking class. The explosion of flavor when we bit into the combination of the nutty baby Autumn greens, crumbled Nauvoo blue cheese, and amazingly complex Freyburg apples was a marriage made in culinary heaven!*

NOTE: *Liz finds a mixture of 3 parts oil to 1 part vinegar about right for this type of salad. Tasting and experimentation will determine your ideal proportions.*

INGREDIENTS

4 quarts of mixed baby salad greens (mizuna, arugula, baby oak leaf, and red tipped lettuce), or substitute the inner leaves of commercial variety lettuces

1 small sweet red onion, peeled and diced

4 ounces of well ripened Nauvoo, or other quality blue cheese, crumbled

3 aromatic, firm-fleshed apples, cored and diced (Freyburgs are Great!)

1/4 cup of Blackberry, or other fruit vinegar (see page 102)

3/4 cup of hazelnut oil

sea salt and freshly ground pepper, to taste

SERVES 12

SHRIMP AND APPLE SALAD
WITH TOASTED SESAME SEED

Preheat oven to 300° F.

(1) Toast the sesame seeds for 20 minutes in oven; set aside to cool.
(2) Slice apples with the corer-wedger, then cut each wedge into four pieces.
(3) In a large bowl, toss together shrimp, apple, celery, sesame seeds, and tarragon.
(4) In another bowl, whisk together mayonnaise, sour cream, and sesame oil.
(5) Pour dressing over salad and mix thoroughly.
(6) Season to taste with sea salt and white pepper.
(7) Cover and chill overnight or at least 2 hours before serving.

NOTE: This salad is pretty garnished with wedges of unpeeled green apples and sprigs of fresh tarragon. Be sure to squeeze a little lemon juice on the apple wedges and toss to coat. This will prevent the apples from discoloring.

INGREDIENTS

1 pound medium shrimp, cooked and cleaned
4 medium tart, green-skinned apples, cored, but not peeled, cut into 1/2-inch dice
1 1/2 cups of celery, diced
1/2 cup of sesame seeds
3 tablespoons of fresh tarragon, minced
1 cup of mayonnaise
1 cup of sour cream
3 tablespoons of sesame oil
sea salt and white pepper to taste

NOTE: This was one of Liz's buffet items in her class on "How to Cater Your Own Wedding." For the budget-minded, the apples and celery allow you to stretch expensive shrimp to feed a crowd.

SERVES 12

BACON APPLE CHEDDAR
CORN STICKS

Preheat oven to 400° F.

(1) Sauté bacon until crisp.
(2) Drain bacon, reserving fat; set bacon dice aside.
(3) Grease 2 7-stick cast iron corn stick molds with some of the reserved bacon fat and place in the oven to heat (this will smoke somewhat, but don't be alarmed. The hot molds make a much crisper corn stick).
(4) Mix the corn meal, flour, baking powder, salt, and sugar.
(5) Stir with a whisk to combine.
(6) Stir in shredded cheese and diced apple.
(7) Lightly whisk eggs and buttermilk together.
(8) Stir into dry ingredients.
(9) Add the reserved bacon fat and crumbled bacon. Do not over-mix.
(10) Remove molds from oven and fill each with some of the batter.
(11) Place molds back in the oven and bake for 20-25 minutes or until golden.

 INGREDIENTS

1/4 pound of bacon, diced
1 cup of corn meal
1 cup of unbleached flour
2 tablespoons of baking powder
1 teaspoon of salt
1 tablespoon of sugar
1 medium red skinned apple, cored and diced but not peeled
1/2 cup of shredded cheddar cheese
2 extra-large eggs
1 cup of buttermilk
1/2 cup of reserved bacon fat

NOTE: How much more American can you get than cast iron stick molds turning out this all-American combination? These are a perennial, along with some of the yeast breads, on Liz's Thanksgiving table. A great, fast accompaniment to a hearty bowl of one of our apple soups!

MAKES 14 CORN STICKS

CRACKED WHEAT AND
APPLE MUFFINS

Preheat oven to 425° F.

(1) Cover cracked wheat cereal with boiling water and set aside for at least 1 hour (preferably overnight).
(2) Sauté apple in 3 tablespoons of butter over medium heat until apple begins to color.
(3) Add thyme. Sauté a few more moments, stirring constantly; set aside to cool.
(4) Spray a 12-muffin tin and a 12-mini muffin tin with non-stick baking spray and set aside.
(5) Sift together the flours, sugar, salt, baking powder, and baking soda.
(6) With a pastry cutter, cut in the remaining 2 tablespoons of butter until fine.
(7) Stir in the cooled wheat cereal and sautéd apple.
(8) Whisk together egg and buttermilk. Stir into cereal mixture until mixture is moistened. Do not overmix or muffins will be tough!
(9) Fill prepared muffin tins 3/4 full and bake in the preheated oven.
(10) Test the mini-muffins after 12 minutes and the large muffins after 25 minutes.

INGREDIENTS

1/2 cup of cracked wheat cereal
1/2 cup of boiling water
1 medium apple cored and diced
1 tablespoon of fresh thyme (1 teaspoon dried)
3 tablespoons of butter
1 cup of unbleached flour
1/2 cup of stone ground whole wheat flour
2 tablespoons of sugar
1 teaspoon of salt
1 teaspoon of baking powder
1/2 teaspoon of baking soda
2 tablespoons of butter
1 extra-large egg
1 cup of buttermilk
non-stick baking spray for coating muffin tins

NOTE: Cracked Wheat Cereal is available by mail order. *(see page 75)*

MAKES 12 LARGE MUFFINS AND 12 MINI-MUFFINS

CINNAMON APPLE SCONES

Preheat oven to 425° F.

(1) In the bowl of an electric mixer fitted with the paddle attachment, combine the flour, sugar, cinnamon, baking powder, baking soda, and salt.

(2) Cut in butter until mixture resembles course meal; add drained apples.

(3) Whisk together 1 egg and yogurt and add to flour mixture. Mix just until flour is moistened.

(4) Turn dough out on a floured surface. Knead lightly until just combined.

(5) Divide dough in half and pat each into circles.

(6) Place dough circles on a buttered baking sheet and score to create 6 equal wedges.

(7) Whisk together the other egg and milk.

(8) Brush scones with egg-wash and sprinkle with sugar.

(9) Place baking sheet on the center shelf and bake for 15 minutes or until golden.

NOTE: Liz's friend, Kay Owen, owner of La Corsette Inn in Newton, Iowa, originated the technique of replacing cream with yogurt.

INGREDIENTS

2 1/2 cups of all purpose flour
1/2 cup of sugar
1/2 teaspoon of cinnamon
2 teaspoons of baking powder
1 teaspoon of baking soda
1/2 teaspoon of salt
4 tablespoons of chilled butter, cut into small pieces
3 tablespoons of finely chopped, dried apple, plumped in simmering cider, then drained (If dried apples are unavailable, substitute raisins or currants.)
1 extra-large egg
1 cup of cinnamon/apple yogurt

Glaze:
1 extra-large egg
1 tablespoon of milk
2 tablespoons of sugar for sprinkling

MAKES 12 SCONES

CARAWAY AND APPLE
RYE BREAD

(1) In the bowl of an electric mixer fitted with the dough hook, proof the yeast in the 1/2 cup of warm water with the sugar.

(2) When the yeast is foaming, add the salt and the remaining 2 cups of warm water. Stir to dissolve the salt.

(3) Add the caraway seed, rye flour and three cups of the unbleached flour. Stir again.

(4) Knead with the dough hook for about 2 minutes.

(5) Add the diced apples and any remaining unbleached flour necessary to make a smooth dough. (This will be a fairly wet dough so do not be alarmed because it does not clean the sides of the bowl.)

(6) Place the dough in a large bowl coated with cooking oil and turn to coat.

(7) Cover with a clean linen towel and place in a warm draft-free place to rise until doubled in bulk.

(8) With a curved plastic bowl-scraper, turn dough out on to a very well floured cloth.

(9) Turn dough to coat with flour.

(10) Divide dough in half. With floured hands shape 2 round loaves.

(11) Spray two 12-inch springform baking pans with non-stick baking spray and sprinkle bottoms with cornmeal. Put loaves in pans. Cover with linen towels and allow to rise for 1 hour.

Preheat oven to 400° F.

(12) Place pans in the oven on the center shelf and bake for about 40 minutes, or until the loaves are browned on top.

(13) Remove springform sides and return loaves to oven for about 10 minutes in order to firm and brown the sides. Loaves should sound hollow when tapped.

(14) Cool on racks.

INGREDIENTS

1 tablespoon of dry yeast
1/2 cup + 2 cups of warm water
 (not more than 115° F.)
1 tablespoon of sugar
1 tablespoon of salt
2 tablespoons of caraway seeds
2 cups of stone ground rye flour
1 cup of stone ground whole
 wheat flour
3-4 cups of unbleached flour
2 firm red apples cored, but not
 peeled, cut into 1/4-inch dice
non-stick baking spray
cornmeal for coating baking pans

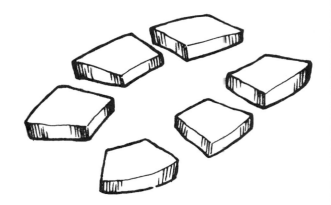

MAKES 2 LOAVES

FRENCH LOAVES

(1) Proof yeast in 1/2 cup of warm water

(2) When yeast is foaming, stir in the additional 2 cups of water.

(3) Add sea salt and sugar and stir to dissolve.

(4) Stir in 5 cups of unbleached flour. Add additional flour, if necessary, to make a stiff but workable dough.

(5) Continue to knead until dough is smooth (about 15 minutes by hand or until the dough cleans the sides of the bowl if using a mixer with a dough hook).

(6) Place the dough in an oiled bowl, turning to coat, and cover with a cloth.

(7) Place in a warm spot and allow to rise until doubled in bulk.

(8) Turn dough out on a floured surface and shape into six baguette sized loaves.

(9) Place loaves on 2 baking sheets that have been greased and sprinkled with corn meal.

(10) Cover and allow to rise again until doubled.

(11) Make diagonal slashes in the top of each loaf and brush with water.

Preheat oven to 400° F.

(12) Place oven racks in the center of the oven. Place baking sheets on separate shelves in the oven and bake for 10 minutes.

(13) Remove from oven and brush with water again. Alternate trays on shelves when replacing.

(14) Repeat twice for a total of 30 minutes baking time.

(15) Remove loaves from oven and cool on racks.

INGREDIENTS

1 tablespoon of dry yeast
1/2 cup + 2 cups of warm water
   (not more than 115° F)
1 tablespoon of sea salt
1 tablespoon of sugar
5-8 cups of unbleached flour

NOTE: *Jill thinks that fresh French
      bread is the ideal palate refresh-
      er for apple tasting parties.
      Unless you live near a great
      bakery, you'll have to learn to
      make your own. Liz's loaves
      are also the perfect complement
      to her soups and pâtés.*

MAKES 6 LOAVES

BACON APPLE
SOURDOUGH LOAVES

(1) Cook the bacon until crisp; drain and reserve fat.

(2) Proof yeast in 1/2 cup of warm water with the sugar.

(3) Stir in the Sourdough Starter

(4) Measure the reserved bacon fat into a 2-cup glass measure and add enough warm water to make 2 cups.

(5) Stir bacon fat into the sourdough mixture.

(6) Add the whole wheat flour and 5 cups of the unbleached flour. Stir to mix. If dough is sticky, add enough of the remaining flour to make a stiff but workable dough.

(7) Knead in the diced bacon and apple.

(8) Continue to knead until dough is smooth (about 15 minutes by hand, or until dough cleans the sides of the bowl, if using a mixer with a dough hook).

(9) Place in an oiled bowl, turning to coat, and cover with a linen towel. Place in a warm spot and allow to rise until doubled in bulk.

(10) Turn dough out on a floured surface, pat into a circle and cut into 4 pieces.

(11) Shape into round loaves and pinch bottoms to seal. Place on two cookie sheets coated with corn meal. Cover and allow to rise again until doubled.

Preheat oven to 400° F.

(12) Place racks in the center of the oven.

(13) Slash the tops of each loaf in a "tic-tac-toe" pattern and place on racks in oven.

(14) Bake for 15 minutes, then alternate cookie sheets and bake another 15 minutes, or until loaves are browned and sound hollow when tapped.

(15) Remove loaves from oven and cool on racks.

INGREDIENTS

1/2 pound of bacon, diced
1 tablespoon of dry yeast
1/2 cup of warm water (not more
    than 115° F.)
1 tablespoon of sugar
1 cup of active Sourdough Starter
    (see box)
1 cup of Nauvoo or other stone
    ground whole wheat flour
5-6 cups of unbleached flour
2 firm, tart apples, cored and diced

*NOTE: Sourdough Starter will keep
indefinitely if fed once a week and
refrigerated between uses. Bring to
room temperature each time you use it.*

SOURDOUGH STARTER

(1) Mix water, yeast, and flour in a
    medium-sized, non-reactive
    (enamel) bowl.
(2) Cover bowl with plastic wrap;
    secure with a rubber band. Let fer-
    ment at room temperature for 4
    days.
(3) Every time you use 1 cup of the
    Starter, add 1 cup of water and 1
    cup of flour.

INGREDIENTS

2 cups of warm water
2 tablespoons of yeast
2 cups of unbleached flour

MAKES 4 LOAVES

73

CHEDDAR PUFFS

Preheat oven to 400° F.

(1) Grease a large cookie sheet with 1 tablespoon of butter and set aside.

(2) In a heavy bottomed pan, over medium high heat, bring water and remaining butter to a boil.

(3) Add flour all at once and stir briskly with a wooden spoon until mixture leaves the sides of the pan.

(4) Continue to stir for about four minutes to cook the flour thoroughly.

(5) Place mixture in the container of a food processor, fitted with the steel blade.

(6) With processor running, add eggs one at a time, through the feed tube.

(7) Remove lid of processor and add salt, sugar, and cheddar cheese.

(8) Process until combined.

(9) Place mixture in a pastry tube, fitted with the plain tip, and pipe out into 1-inch mounds on the sheet.

(10) Bake for 12-15 minutes, or until

 INGREDIENTS

9 tablespoons of butter
1 cup of water
1 cup of flour
4 extra-large eggs
1 teaspoon of salt
1 teaspoon of sugar
1/2 cup of shredded cheddar cheese

puffed and golden.

(11) Remove to a rack to cool.

(12) Repeat until all batter is used.

NOTE: This is Liz's Americanized version of the classic Burgundian Gougere. Jill says that cheddar puffs can elevate a simple menu of soup and apples to epic heights. They're also great served with apple wedges as an appetizer.

MAKES ABOUT 50 PUFFS

APPLESAUCE BREAD

(1) Proof yeast in the 1/2 cup of warm water.

(2) Mix the applesauce and the remaining cup of warm water together.

(3) Add to the yeast mixture and stir.

(4) Mix in the whole wheat flour, bran flour, and 3 cups of the unbleached flour. Stir to combine.

(5) Follow steps 8 through 15 of Bacon Apple Sourdough Loaves on page 72.

NOTE: *Stone ground whole wheat flour is available from Nauvoo Mill and Bakery, 1530 Mulholland Street, Nauvoo, IL 62354 (217-453-6734)*

INGREDIENTS

1 tablespoon of dry yeast

1/2 cup of warm water (not more than 115° F.)

1 cup of fresh applesauce (see page 37)

1 cup of warm water (not more than 115° F.)

1 tablespoon of salt

2 cups of Nauvoo (see note) or other stone ground whole wheat flour

1 cup of bran flour

3-5 cups of unbleached flour

MAKES 4 LOAVES

APPLE WALNUT
WHOLE WHEAT BREAD

(1) In the bowl of an electric mixer, fitted with the dough hook, proof the yeast in the 1/2 cup of warm water with the sugar.

(2) When the yeast is foaming, add the salt and the remaining 2 cups of warm water.

(3) Stir to dissolve the salt.

(4) Add the whole wheat flour and 3 cups of the unbleached flour.

(5) Stir to mix, then add apples and walnuts.

(6) Knead with the dough hook, adding as much of the remaining flour as necessary for the dough to form a smooth mass that cleans the sides of the bowl.

(7) Place the dough in a large bowl coated with cooking oil and turn to coat.

(8) Cover with a clean linen towel and place in a warm, draft-free place to rise until doubled in bulk.

(9) Turn dough out on a floured surface and pat out into a circle about 1-inch thick.

(10) Cut into 4 pieces. Pinch corners of each piece together to form a round loaves.

(11) Coat tops of each loaf with flour.

(12) Place loaves, pinched side down on baking sheets, sprayed with non-stick baking spray

🍎 INGREDIENTS

1 tablespoon of dry yeast

1/2 cup + 2 cups of warm water (not more than 115° F)

1 tablespoon of sugar

1 tablespoon of salt

2 cups of Nauvoo, or other stone-ground whole wheat flour

3-4 cups of unbleached flour

2 firm red apples, cored, but not peeled and cut into 1/2 inch dice

1 cup of walnut pieces

non-stick baking spray

cornmeal

---

and sprinkled with cornmeal.

(13) Cover loaves with linen towels and allow to rise again for about 1 hour.

(14) Slash tops of loaves with a sharp knife.

Preheat oven to 400° F.

(15) Place loaves in oven; bake for 30 minutes or until they sound hollow when tapped. Cool on racks.

MAKES 4 LOAVES

APPLE DUMPLINGS

Preheat oven to 400° F.

(1) **Quick Tip:** Loosen the wing nut and drop the coring-slicing blade. Peel the apples on "the machine." Core the whole, peeled apples with the apple-corer.

(2) Place peeled and cored apples in an enameled pan large enough to hold them.

(3) Add the red candies and water to cover.

(4) Simmer the apples until they are just barely tender when pierced with the point of a knife. Drain.

(5) Roll out the puff pastry on a floured cloth to form a sheet approximately 18x24-inches.

(6) Cut the pastry into 6 squares large enough to completely enclose each apple.

(7) Place an apple in the center of each pastry square.

(8) Put 2 caramels in each apple.

(9) Brush the edges of the pastry with the egg wash.

(10) Bring four corners of the pastry together in the center to form a square package.

INGREDIENTS

1 recipe No-Fail Puff Pastry (see page 95)

6 small firm, sweet apples, peeled and cored

2/3 cup of red cinamon-flavored candies

12 square caramel candies, cellophane removed

1 egg beaten with 1 tablespoon of water

granulated sugar for sprinkling

(11) Pinch seams together to seal them.

(12) Place packages seam side up on a baking sheet.

(13) Brush the tops of the packages with more of the egg wash and sprinkle with the granulated sugar.

(14) Place in the oven and bake for about 15 minutes or until pastry is puffed and browned.

(15) Serve immediately.

SERVES 6

MAPLE CREAM
CHEESE FROSTING

(1) Place cream cheese, butter, sugar, vanilla extract, and maple flavoring in the bowl of a mixer fitted with paddle attachment.
(2) Mix until completely smooth and combined.

MAKES ENOUGH FROSTING FOR BOTH PANS OF BARS
(see page 81)

 INGREDIENTS

8 ounces of cream cheese, at room temperature
8 tablespoons of unsalted butter, at room temperature
3 cups of powdered sugar
1 teaspoon of vanilla extract
1/2 teaspoon of maple flavoring

LEMON SAUCE

(1) In a heavy-bottomed sauce pan, preferably one with a non-stick finish, melt butter over medium high heat.
(2) Add sugar and stir to dissolve.
(3) Allow to caramelize, stirring constantly.
(4) When sugar is golden brown, pour in lemon juice.
(5) Mixture will boil furiously and sugar will seize. Don't be alarmed.
(6) Continue to stir and sugar will re-melt and sauce will thicken.

 INGREDIENTS

4 tablespoon of unsalted butter
1 cup of sugar
1/2 cup of lemon juice

NOTE: Serve with Apple and Cranberry Bread Pudding (see page 82)

MAKES ABOUT 1 CUP

CINNAMON CANDY
STEWED APPLES

(1) **Quick Trick:** Peel the apples on "the machine," then cut with the corer-wedger for thick crescents.

(2) Place the apple wedges in a large enameled Dutch oven.

(3) Add the water and the cinnamon candies.

(4) Place the Dutch oven over medium high heat and bring to a boil; stirring constantly.

(5) Reduce heat to medium and continue to stir until candies are dissolved and apples are soft but not mushy.

(6) If too much liquid remains, raise heat and boil until 1/2 cup remains. The more concentrated the liquid, the more intense the color and flavor of the apples.

(7) Serve warm or at room temperature.

NOTE: *When Liz started the recipe development for this book, the one request for a dish that men immediately came up with was the "red hot" or cinnamon candy apples they remembered from*

🍎 INGREDIENTS

8 large firm apples, cored, wedged, and peeled

1 1/2 cups of water

9 ounces of red cinnamon-flavored candies

---

their childhood. It seems that most mothers did this dish throughout the fall. Liz remembers it from her own childhood being there as an after-school snack when she came home to the farm. The problem with testing the recipe is no one's mother, including Liz's, wrote it down! This is Liz's version, as best memory serves her, forty years later! Eat it "after school," as a nostalgic accompaniment to a family Thanksgiving or Christmas dinner, or cold for breakfast! An instant trip back to childhood!

SERVES 8

ESTHER'S OZARK PUDDING

Preheat oven to 325° F.

(1) Whip egg whites in a mixing bowl fitted with the balloon whip until stiff but not dry; set aside.

(2) Combine sugar and egg yolks and beat with the paddle attachment until lemon colored and thick.

(3) Peel, core, and slice the apples on the machine. Press the corer-wedger over the spiral to form uniform small dice.

(4) Add apples and remaining ingredients to egg mixture; mix well.

(5) Fold the beaten egg whites into the mixture.

(6) Lightly oil a 13x8x2-inch baking pan.

(7) Spread the mixture in the pan, smoothing it with a spatula.

(8) Bake 35-40 minutes.

NOTE: *In the 1950's, Liz's Aunt Esther came across this recipe, reputed to be Harry Truman's favorite dessert, which was then making the rounds. Esther served it up at a Sunday family dinner. Though using commonly available local ingredients, the preparation was just exotic enough to make this meringue-like dessert special.*

INGREDIENTS

4 extra-large eggs, separated
1 1/2 cups of sugar
1/2 cup of flour
1/4 teaspoon of salt
1 teaspoon of baking powder
2 large, tart apples peeled and finely diced
1 cup of chopped hickory nuts

NOTE: *Unless you have access to a "little old lady" who picks out hickory nuts, they are a luxury of the past. In that case, substitute pecans.*

SERVES 8

DATE AND APPLE BARS

Preheat oven to 350° F.

(1) Place all the flour, sugar, baking powder, and salt in the bowl of a mixer.
(2) Stir thoroughly with a wire whisk to combine them.
(3) Add dates, apples, and pecans, and mix them in.
(4) Add melted butter and eggs.
(5) With the paddle attachment of the mixer, beat the batter until completely combined.
(6) Lightly oil two 13x8x2-inch baking pans.
(7) Spread the batter evenly in both pans.
(8) Place the pans on the center shelf of the oven.
(9) Bake for about 25 minutes, or until a toothpick inserted in the center comes out clean.
(10) Cool and cut into bars.
(11) Spread with Maple Cream Cheese Frosting if desired. (see page 78)

INGREDIENTS

2 cups of unbleached flour
2 cups of sugar
1/2 teaspoon of baking powder
1 teaspoon of salt
1 cup of chopped dates
1 1/2 cups of chopped dried apples
1 1/2 cups of chopped pecans
1/2 cup of butter melted and cooled
4 eggs beaten

NOTE: *This recipe can save your sanity on one of those evenings when the announcement comes at 8:30 PM, "Oh, by the way, Mom, I need 4 dozen cookies for the speech team bake sale tomorrow"! Quickly put together from ingredients kept available on the shelf, the bars can be mixed and baked in about half an hour.*

MAKES ABOUT 50 BARS

APPLE AND CRANBERRY
BREAD PUDDING

Preheat oven to 350° F.

(1) Place bread and 2 cups of sugar in a mixing bowl.
(2) Pour milk over and mix well. Allow bread to soak up milk for about an hour.
(3) In a non-reactive (enamel) saucepan, combine 1 cup of sugar and the cranberries.
(4) Cover with water and simmer for a 1/2 hour; set aside to cool.
(5) Whisk together eggs, cinnamon, nutmeg, vanilla extract, rum, and melted butter.
(6) Pour over bread crumbs.
(7) Cut apples into wedges with the corer-wedger, then cut each wedge into four large chunks.
(8) Stir in apples, walnuts, and cranberries drained of their cooking liquid into egg mixture.
(9) Pour entire mixture into a baking dish large enough to hold it. (An enameled cast iron pan with a non-stick finish is ideal).

🍎 INGREDIENTS

4 cups of stale bread, cubed
2 cups of sugar
2 cups of milk
1 cup of sugar
1/2 pound fresh cranberries
4 eggs
cinnamon and freshly grated nutmeg to taste
1 tablespoon of vanilla extract
3 tablespoon of rum (Meyers dark preferred)
3/4 cup of melted butter, cooled
2 firm, tart apples, cored and chunked but not peeled
1/2 cup of walnut halves
Lemon Sauce (see page 78)

(10) Bake for about 30 minutes, or until puffed and golden.
(11) Cool slightly, cut into squares, and serve with lemon sauce.

SERVES 8

CHEWY APPLE AND PECAN
COOKIES

Preheat oven to 350° F.

(1) Cream butter, brown sugar, and sugar together in the bowl of an electric mixer.
(2) When completely combined, add vanilla extract and eggs. Mix until lemony.
(3) Place oatmeal into blender or food processor and process until powdered.
(4) In another bowl, sift together oatmeal, flour, baking powder, salt, and baking soda.
(5) Gradually add dry ingredients into the mixer bowl; beat on low speed until combined.
(6) Place Hershey bar in blender or food processor. Process until powdered.
(7) Cut the apples with the corer-wedger, then cut each wedge into four large chunks.
(8) Add grated Hershey bar, apples, and pecans and mix in.
(9) Grease a cookie sheet.
(10) Using an ice cream scoop, evenly place nine cookies on the sheet.
(11) Bake for about 10 minutes, more if desired. Ideally, the cookie should be just barely brown on the edges and still very

INGREDIENTS

1 cup of unsalted butter
1 cup of lightly packed brown sugar
1 cup of granulated sugar
1 teaspoon of vanilla extract
2 extra-large eggs
2 1/2 cups of oatmeal
2 cups of unbleached flour
1 teaspoon each of salt, baking powder, and baking soda
4 ounces of Hershey's milk chocolate bars or morsels
3 tart, red apples, cored but not peeled, cut into 1/2 inch chunks
1 cup of pecan halves

---

soft when removed from the oven.
(12) With a wide spatula remove cookies to a rack.
(13) Cool cookie sheet, then grease again and repeat until all dough is used.

MAKES ABOUT 24 COOKIES

APPLE AND RAISIN
BROWN SUGAR PIE

Preheat oven to 375° F.

(1) Divide pie crust recipe into 4 balls. (Freeze 2 for later use.)

(2) Roll out 1 of the balls 1/8-inch thick and fit into a Pyrex 10-inch pie plate. (Use the rolling pin as an aid, drape the crust over the pin and gently unfold it into the pie plate.)

(3) Trim excess crust with a sharp knife.

(4) ***Quick Trick:*** Run the apples through the peeler/corer/slicer. Cut one diameter through the spiral to form uniform thin rainbows.

(5) In a large bowl, toss together the apples and raisins.

(6) Sprinkle the brown sugar, flour, and cinnamon over the fruit and toss with your hands to evenly coat each piece.

(7) Pour the fruit into the pie pan.

Scatter the bits of butter over the fruit.

(8) Roll out the second ball of pie dough 1/8-inch thick and again using the rolling pin to aid, drape the top crust over the pie.

(9) Crimp the top and bottom crusts together with a fork or your fingers. Cut vents in the top crust to allow steam to escape.

(10) Cut designs such as leaves and apples from the scraps of dough if desired.

(11) Combine egg and 1 tablespoon of water.

(12) Brush the top crust with the egg wash.

(13) Attach any pastry decorations, and brush the tops.

(14) Place the pie on a cookie sheet with sides to catch any run-over and place in the oven and bake for 45-60 minutes or until juices are bubbling and crust is golden.

(15) Allow to cool at least 30 minutes before slicing.

NOTE: *The best pies - like the best applesauce and cider - often result from combining more than one variety. Jill's favorite combination is Jonathan apples with one McIntosh added for aroma. Another popular combination is Melrose and Mutsu.*

 INGREDIENTS

1 recipe "Old-Fashioned Pie Crust" (see page 94)

6 medium tart apples, peeled and sliced

1/2 cup of raisins, simmered in bourbon, brandy, or water for 5 minutes, then drained

1/2 - 3/4 cup of loosely packed brown sugar, depending upon the sweetness of the apples

4 tablespoons of flour

1/2 teaspoon of cinnamon

3 tablespoons of unsalted butter, cut into bits

1 extra-large egg

1 tablespoon of water

SERVES 8

POACHED APPLES
WITH BRANDY SABAYON

Preheat oven to 300° F.

(1) Remove a thin slice from the top and bottom of each apple, but leave the stem intact.

(2) Peel the apple vertically to form facets.

(3) Using an apple corer, carefully remove the bottom 2/3 of the core and all of the seeds.

(4) Place the apples in an enameled pan just large enough to hold them all in one layer.

(5) Add enough apple cider to cover.

(6) Stir in the 1 cup of sugar and the vanilla extract.

(7) Bring the cider slowly to a boil then reduce heat to a simmer and poach until the apples are tender, but not mushy, when pierced with a sharp knife.

(8) Drain and cool apples, reserving liquid.

(9) While the apples are poaching, prepare the filling. Place the walnut pieces on a cookie sheet and lightly toast in the oven for 15 minutes.

(10) In a food processor fitted with the steel blade, combine 1/4 cup of the walnuts, blue cheese, ricotta cheese, and 1/3 cup of sugar and process to a smooth paste.

(11) Remove cheese mixture from processor and divide into six equal portions.

(12) Gently roll cheese portions into cylinders and set aside.

(13) Prepare the Sabayon just before serving. Bring 2 inches of water to a boil in the bottom half of a double boiler.

(14) In the top half, whisk together the egg yolks, 1/2 cup of sugar, brandy or cognac, and reserved poaching cider.

(15) Remove the top half and reduce the heat under the double boiler until the water is just simmering.

(16) Place the top half back on top of the simmering water and whisk the egg yolk mixture until it is foamy and doubled in volume.

(17) To serve, place the cylinders of cheese mixture in the hollow of each poached apple.
(18) Set apples upright in deep individual serving dishes or bubble wine glasses.
(19) Pour warm Sabayon over apples, sprinkle with reserved walnuts and serve.

NOTE: Liz developed this recipe for the Heartland Harvest Festival in the fall of 1987 sponsored by the Heartland Food Society in Chicago. In this elegant recipe, Liz uses the classic French method of hand-peeling the apple to form vertical "facets." This cutting method can be used wherever you want a "formally-attired" whole, peeled, cored apple.

 INGREDIENTS

6 large tart, firm apples
8 cups of apple cider (preferably unpasteurized)
1 cup of sugar
1 teaspoon of vanilla extract

Filling

1/2 cup of walnut pieces
1/2 cup of blue cheese
1/2 cup of ricotta cheese
1/3 cup of sugar

Sabayon Sauce

6 extra-large egg yolks
1/2 cup of sugar
1/4 cup of brandy or cognac
3/4 cup of the cooled cider used to poach the apples.

SERVES 6

OVEN APPLE PANCAKE
(FRENCH CLAFOUTIS)

Preheat oven to 400° F.

(1) Spray a fluted porcelain dish with the nonstick spray.
(2) Arrange the apple slices evenly around the baking dish.
(3) Combine the flour, sugar, eggs, milk, vanilla, and cinnamon in the container of a blender; process until smooth.
(4) Pour the batter over the apples.
(5) Bake on the center shelf of the preheated oven for 25 minutes or until puffed and browned.
(6) Sift confectioners' sugar on top of the pancake.
(7) Cut into wedges.
(8) Serve with Calvados or brandy-flavored whipped cream as an accompaniment.

 INGREDIENTS

1 large apple, cored, peeled, and thinly sliced
1 cup of all-purpose flour
1/2 cup of sugar
3 extra-large eggs
1 cup of milk
1 teaspoon of vanilla
1/2 teaspoon of cinnamon
non-stick baking spray
Confectioners' sugar for sifting, if desired

NOTE: *This is one of the most versatile of fruit desserts. If you only have one apple, this recipe will allow you to stretch it into a dessert worthy of being served at a dinner party.*

SERVES 8

APPLE PANCAKE
(ITALIAN TORTA DI MELE)

(1) Whisk together flour, eggs, sugar, vanilla powder or extract, cream, and water. Mixture should resemble thick cream.

(2) Cut the apples with the corer-wedger. Peel each wedge then slice it lengthwise into three thin crescents.

(3) Stir apples into mixture.

(4) In a heavy skillet, preferably with a non-stick finish, melt enough butter to coat the pan when pan is tilted.

(5) Pour batter into skillet and cook pancake over medium heat.

(6) As mixture begins to set, lift the edges with a flexible spatula to allow uncooked batter to run underneath.

(7) Preheat broiler.

(8) When pancake begins to brown and firm, place the entire skillet under the broiler to puff and brown.

(9) Sprinkle with additional sugar.

(10) Cut into 8 wedges and serve.

 INGREDIENTS

1 cup of unbleached all-purpose flour
4 extra-large eggs
3 tablespoons of sugar
Dash vanilla powder or extract
1/2 cup of heavy whipping cream
1/2 cup of water
2 apples, thinly sliced
butter

NOTE: This technique comes from Albertina Guliani, the mother in the Italian family where Liz was an exchange student in the 1960's.

NOTE: Do not use a wooden handled skillet.

SERVES 8

APPLE AND BROWN SUGAR
ICE CREAM

(1) **Quick Trick:** Run the apples through the peeler/corer/slicer. Cut through the spiral with the corer-wedger to form small, uniform dice.

(2) Combine apples, brown sugar, water, vanilla extract, brandy or cognac, and cinnamon in an enameled sauce pan.

(3) Bring to a boil and simmer until apples are soft; remove from heat and cool.

(4) Purée apple mixture in the bowl of a food processor fitted with the steel blade.

(5) Add whipping cream.

(6) Pour apple mixture into the container of an ice cream maker and freeze according to manufacturer's directions.

INGREDIENTS

6 firm-fleshed tart apples, cored, peeled, and diced
1 cup of dark brown sugar, loosely packed
1 1/2 cups of water
1 teaspoon of vanilla extract
1/4 cup of brandy or cognac
1/2 teaspoon of cinnamon
1 cup of heavy whipping cream

SERVES 8

APPLE, LAVENDER AND LEMON THYME
ICE CREAM

(1) In a heavy 2-quart sauce pan, place the water, sugar, lavender, and lemon thyme.

(2) Bring to a boil and then remove from heat. Allow herbs to steep in the sugar syrup for at least 1 hour, or overnight, if possible.

(3) Strain herbs from sugar syrup and discard.

(4) **Quick Trick:** Run the apples through the peeler/corer/slicer. Cut one diameter through the spiral to form rainbows.

(5) Return syrup to pan. Add apple slices.

(6) Simmer over medium low heat until apples begin to disintegrate; adding a bit more water if syrup level begins to get low. Cool mixture.

(7) Place apples and syrup in the container of a blender.

(8) Add vanilla extract and cream. Process until puréed.

(9) Pour mixture into the container of an ice cream maker, and freeze according to manufacturer's directions.

INGREDIENTS

1 cup of sugar
1 cup of water
4 large sprigs of lemon thyme
3 3-inch sprigs of lavender
3 tart, firm apples, peeled, cored, and sliced
1 teaspoon of vanilla extract
1 cup of heavy whipping cream

SERVES 6

CARAMELIZED APPLE
GINGERBREAD

Preheat oven to 350° F.

(1) Peel whole apples with a vegetable peeler.

(2) Cut the apples in half lengthwise (from stem end to blossom end).

(3) ***Quick Trick:*** Using a pear-corer, remove the stem and scoop out a round depression. When you remove the core, cut out the end pieces of core with the v-shaped end of the pear corer.

(4) Place the apples in an enameled pan large enough to hold them in one layer.

(5) Add sugar, vanilla extract, and water to cover.

(6) Bring to a boil over medium high heat, reduce heat; and simmer until apples are just beginning to soften, but still retain their shape, about 8-10 minutes.

(7) With a slotted spoon, remove apples from poaching liquid and reserve.

(8) Melt the butter in a 9x1 1/2-inch non-stick round cake pan on a low burner.

(9) Add the corn syrup and brown sugar.

(10) Stir with a wooden spoon until sugar is completely melted. Remove from heat.

(11) Fill the depression of each apple half with as many of the walnut or pecan pieces as it will hold.

(12) Gently turn the apple halves flat side down on the caramel mixture, keeping the nut meats in place.

(13) Sprinkle any remaining nuts around and between the apples.

(14) In the bowl of an electric mixer, fitted with the paddle attachment, cream the butter and sugar until lemony.

(15) Add the egg and mix until completely combined.

(16) Mix in the molasses.

(17) Sift together the flour, baking powder, baking soda, cinnamon, and ginger.

(18) Add the dry ingredients and sour cream to the batter and mix thoroughly.

(19) When batter is smooth, pour over apples and level with a spatula.

(20) Place cake pan on the center rack of the oven and bake for 50 minutes to 1

hour. (After 50 minutes test with a toothpick. Gingerbread is finished when toothpick comes out clean.)

(21) Remove from oven and cool on a rack for 10-15 minutes.

(22) Invert gingerbread on a serving platter.

(23) Cut into wedges and serve with Crème Fraíche (see page 105) or lightly sweetened whipped cream.

NOTE: When Liz began researching the recipes for this book, she opened her mother's recipe file boxes, untouched in the nearly 15 years since her mother's death. Many of the recipe cards were in her grandmother's handwriting, and clippings from the 30's and 40's were fragile but still intact. In the file was the recipe for this gingerbread. Though Liz's mother used sour milk, obviously a use for the surplus dairy products accumulated during the war years at the farm, Liz substituted sour cream with no noticeable change from the original. Elegant in appearance, old-fashioned in taste, it's the perfect autumn dinner party dessert.

INGREDIENTS

3 small firm apples
1/2 cup of granulated sugar (more or less to taste, depending on sweetness of apples)
1 teaspoon of vanilla extract
water to cover

2 tablespoons of lightly salted butter
1/4 cup of corn syrup
1/4 cup of brown sugar
6 tablespoons of English walnuts or pecans (pieces)

6 tablespoons of lightly salted butter (slightly softened)
1/2 cup of sugar
1 extra-large egg
2/3 cup of dark molasses
2 cups of unbleached flour
2 teaspoons of baking powder
1/2 teaspoon of baking soda
1 1/2 teaspoons of cinnamon
2 teaspoons of ground ginger
3/4 cup of sour cream

SERVES 12

OLD-FASHIONED PIE CRUST

(1) In the bowl of an electric mixer, fitted with the paddle, place flour, sugar, and salt. Mix a few times to combine.
(2) Add lard and cut in by mixing at low speed.
(3) Combine beaten egg, vinegar, and enough ice water to make 1/2 cup of liquid.
(4) Pour egg mixture slowly into flour and lard with mixer running.
(5) When combined, stop mixer and remove dough.
(6) Divide into 4 balls, wrap in plastic and refrigerate for at least 20 minutes.

NOTE: If dough becomes too cold to roll out easily, cut into 1-inch chunks with a sharp knife and process in a food processor, fitted with the steel blade. Add a teaspoon or more of water, if necessary. Dough will form a ball that can be easily rolled on a floured pastry cloth.

INGREDIENTS

4 cups of sifted flour
1 tablespoon of sugar
1 1/2 teaspoons of salt
1 1/2 cups of lard, at room temperature
1 egg
1 tablespoon of vinegar
ice water

NOTE: This recipe comes from Liz's college roommate's next door neighbor's husband's grandmother! Here, passed on to you, a crust guaranteed to get raves!

MAKES 4 CRUSTS

NO-FAIL PUFF PASTRY

(1) Put the flour, salt, and one stick of the butter, cut into small pieces, into the bowl of a food processor fitted with the steel blade.

(2) Process until the mixture resembles corn meal.

(3) With the motor running add the cold water through the feed tube until the mixture forms a ball and leaves the sides of the bowl.

(4) Turn the dough out onto a floured pastry cloth and roll out into a rough rectangle about 12x16-inches.

(5) Cut the remaining stick of butter into thirds and refrigerate 2/3 of it.

(6) Cut the first 1/3 into pea-sized pieces and distribute over the surface of the dough. Work quickly to avoid having the warmth of your hands melt the butter.

(7) Use the pastry cloth to help fold the dough like a business letter, 1/3 over 1/3, with the butter enclosed.

(8) Now turn the length of pastry and fold 1/3 over 1/3 to make a compact

 INGREDIENTS

2 cups of Wondra Flour
1 teaspoon of salt
2 sticks (1 cup) unsalted, chilled butter
1/2 to 3/4 cup very cold water

package.

(9) Put pastry in a plastic bag and refrigerate for at least 15 minutes. (Do not place in freezer to accelerate chilling.)

(10) Roll at right angles to your rectangle - do not roll diagonally or your butter will not be evenly distributed and you may break through at the corners of the dough.

(11) Repeat from step 6 two more times with the second and third pieces of butter.

(12) At this point the pastry may be used or frozen to reserve for future use.

BAKED APPLE
WITH RASPBERRY PRESERVES

Preheat oven to 350° F.

(1) **Quick Trick:** Core apples from the stem end with apple corer but don't cut completely through to the bottom. Use the small end of a melon baller to scoop out any bits of core left by the corer leaving the outside intact.

(2) Using a pastry brush, coat each apple with some of the egg white.

(3) Place the apples in a heavy, non-stick roasting pan.

(4) Fill the center of each apple with raspberry preserves.

(5) Generously sprinkle the dish with sugar.

(6) Bake for about 45 minutes, or until apples are soft, but still intact.

(7) Remove roasting pan from oven and set on a rack to cool.

(8) Serve at room temperature.

 INGREDIENTS

12 firm tart apples
2 extra-large egg whites, lightly beaten
raspberry preserves, homemade or top quality commercial
sugar for sprinkling

NOTE: For many years, Liz has visited the tiny Hotel Clarion, in the village of Aloxe-Corton, France. Tranquil against the vineyards of the legendary Cote d' Ore, the hotel serves a fantastic breakfast around the lily pond on sunny mornings or in the salon, dominated by a huge carved stone mantle, on less clement days. One damp, chilly morning, June 1993, Liz and Eloise Walther were served one of the best baked apples you've ever eaten. Though served for breakfast, Liz passes it on to you as a dessert, equally good morning or evening.

SERVES 12

APPLE TART

Preheat oven to 375° F.

(1) Divide pastry into fourths. Refrigerate or freeze 3 of the pastry balls and save for another use.
(2) Roll out one of the balls on a floured cloth.
(3) Using the rolling pin to help you, lift the pastry. Line a tart pan with a removable bottom with the pastry.
(4) *Quick Trick:* Run the apples through the peeler/corer/slicer. Cut one diameter through the spiral to form rainbows. Use the uniform, larger slices for the tart.
(5) Spiral the slices, laying them all in the same direction, around the tart shell, beginning in the center and completely covering the bottom of the shell.
(6) Whisk together the eggs, cream, sugar, and vanilla extract.

INGREDIENTS

1 recipe "Old-Fashioned Pie Crust" (see page 94)
4-5 large firm, flavorful apples
4 extra-large eggs
1 cup of heavy whipping cream
3/4 cup of sugar
1 teaspoon of vanilla extract

(7) Carefully pour the mixture over the apples, being sure not to over-flow the tart shell.
(8) Place tart pan on a baking sheet and bake in the oven until puffed and golden; about 45 minutes.

NOTE: *Reserve the smaller end-slices for applesauce or another use.*

SERVES 8

APPLE TART
WITH WALNUTS IN PUFF PASTRY

Preheat oven to 400° F.

(1) Roll pastry out on a floured surface to a thickness of 1/8 inch.

(2) With a sharp knife, cut pastry in half. Refold one half, wrap in plastic and freeze for another purpose.

(3) Measure a rectangle 14x4-inches and cut with a sharp knife.

(4) Using a straight edge, cut three strips, 1/2 inch wide, for each side of rectangle.

(5) Place rectangle of pastry on a cookie sheet.

(6) Brush a coating of the egg wash around the perimeter of the rectangle.

(7) Lay one of the strips over the egg wash on each side.

(8) Brush the tops of the strips with the egg wash and layer again.

(9) Overlap the corners of the strips and continue to build "Lincoln Log Fashion"; using all of the strips.

(10) Using the back of a knife blade, press a lattice pattern into the top strip of pastry.

(11) Brush the final layer with the egg wash.

(12) Cut apples with the corer-wedger. Peel each wedge and halve each wedge lengthwise to form thin crescents.

(13) Lay the apple slices, overlapping like dominos, down the center of the pastry shell.

(14) Sprinkle the walnuts over the apples.

(15) Top the apples and walnuts with the vanilla sugar.

(16) Bake in the oven for 30 to 35 minutes, or until pastry is puffed and golden and sugar has formed a glaze.

(17) Allow tart to cool slightly and slice with a serrated knife.

(18) Serve accompanied by a spoonful of Crème Fraíche. (see page 105)

INGREDIENTS

1 recipe No-Fail Puff Pastry (see page 95)

1 extra-large egg mixed with 1 tablespoon of water for glaze

2-3 large firm-fleshed apples, quartered, peeled, and sliced

1/4 cup of chopped walnuts

1/4 cup of vanilla sugar

SERVES 8

WARM COMPOTE OF
WINTER FRUITS

(1) Place the fruit in a heavy, non-reactive kettle. (an enameled cast iron Dutch oven).
(2) Cover with water.
(3) Bring to a boil over medium-high heat. Reduce heat and simmer. Cook until fruit is reconstituted and soft, about 30 minutes.
(4) Add sugar, cinnamon, cloves, and rum; simmer for 1 hour. If liquid reduces too much, add more water, 1 cup at a time. Fruit should be thick, but slightly liquid.

NOTE: Serve over Apple Brown Sugar Ice Cream (see page 90) or toasted pound cake, or topped with whipped cream flavored with brown sugar and a bit of dark rum and toasted slivered almonds.

NOTE: This versatile fruit compote will keep indefinitely, if covered and refrigerated. Add a bit of liquid to re-warm.

INGREDIENTS

3 pounds of mixed dried fruits (Try to include an assortment of apples, apricots, peaches, pears, and prunes.)
water to cover
1/2 cup of dark brown sugar, loosely packed
4 2-inch pieces of cinnamon stick
1/4 teaspoon of ground cloves
1/2 cup of dark rum

MAKES ABOUT 4 QUARTS OF FRUIT

VANILLA SUGAR

(1) Put sugar in a screw-top quart jar and bury vanila bean in it.
(2) Put lid on jar.
(3) Leave vanilla bean in sugar and shake from time to time, for one week.

NOTE: Vanilla flavor will intensify as it sits. As sugar is used, replace with an equal quantity.

 INGREDIENTS

4 cups of granulated sugar
1 vanilla bean, split in half lengthwise

MAKES 4 CUPS

HERB-INFUSED OLIVE OIL

(1) Place several sprigs of the herb of your choice (clean and dry) into a bottle of extra-virgin olive oil.
(2) Allow to rest for at least 5 days before using. Flavor intensifies as time goes on.

NOTE: This is a real dividend to have on your shelf. It can sauce salads or baste meats or fish when grilling.

 INGREDIENTS

1 pint of extra-virgin olive oil
4 3-inch sprigs of fresh herbs

MAKES 1 PINT

HERBED VINEGAR

(1) In an enameled pan bring vinegar to the boiling point.
(2) Place herbs in a plastic or glass bowl.
(3) Pour hot vinegar over herbs and allow to steep overnight.
(4) Strain vinegar and pour into sterilized bottles; cork. Will keep refrigerated indefinitely.
(5) Add a sprig of fresh herbs to a bottle to give as a gift.

NOTE: *Clear, herbed vinegar can be made by inserting sprigs of the herb into room temperature vinegar and allowing to sit for several weeks. Replace the sprigs with fresh herbs when giving as a gift. (This vinegar will never have the intensity or flavor of the one that is made by heating and steeping.)*

 INGREDIENTS

1 quart of good quality white wine vinegar
1 cup of fresh herbs of your choice (tarragon, rosemary, thyme, etc.)

NOTE: *Fruit vinegars are made in the same way. Put fresh fruit (raspberries, blueberries, cherries, etc.) in the bottle when using for a gift.*

ABOUT 1 QUART

ROSEMARY AND NASTURTIUM
JELLY

(1) Melt jelly in an enameled pan over low heat.

(2) Add rosemary and nasturtium leaves and simmer for 15 minutes.

(3) Allow mixture to cool, watching closely.

(4) When it is just jelling and is completely cool, pour 1/3 of the mixture back into the jar, or into another suitable container.

(5) Press one of the blossoms gently into the jar, taking care to keep the petals open.

(6) Cover with more of the jelly mixture and continue until all blossoms are used and jar is full.

(7) Serve with scones or biscuits for breakfast or tea.

INGREDIENTS

1 pound jar of good-quality apple jelly (homemade is great if you're a jelly-maker)

2 tablespoons of chopped fresh rosemary

6-8 nasturtium leaves, finely chopped

6-8 nasturtium blossoms, stems removed

NOTE: This makes a lovely Christmas or hostess gift when packed in a decorative glass or crystal jam jar.

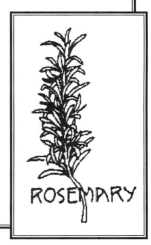

ROSEMARY

LAVENDER AND SCENTED GERANIUM JELLY

(1) Melt the jelly over low heat.
(2) Add the lavender and one of the scented geranium leaves, finely minced.
(3) Allow to simmer for about 10 minutes.
(4) Remove from heat and cool slightly.
(5) Pour about 1 inch of the jelly back into the jar or into another container of choice.
(6) Top with one of the scented geranium leaves.
(7) Cool slightly.
(8) Continue layering in this manner until all of the geranium leaves are used.
(9) Refrigerate.
(10) Serve with biscuits or scones. A delightful accompaniment to tea.

🍎 INGREDIENTS

1 pound jar of apple jelly
4 2-inch sprigs of lavender, minced (see note)
5 or 6 leaves of the scented geranium of your choice (lemon, lime, or other fruit scents all work well)

NOTE: Use only fresh lavender. Most imported dried lavender has been treated with chemicals to meet U.S.D.A. requirements.

MAKES 1 POUND

HARVEST BUTTER

(1) In the container of a food processor fitted with the steel blade, combine butter, cream cheese, and apple-butter.
(2) Process until completely combined and smooth.
(3) Pack the butter into bowls or crocks, cover with plastic wrap; refrigerate.

NOTE: A lovely spread for any of the apple breads, this butter will keep well in the refrigerator.

 INGREDIENTS

1 pound of lightly salted butter, softened
1 8-ounce package of cream cheese, softened
3/4 cup of thick apple-butter

MAKES 3 1/2 CUPS

CRÈME FRAÍCHE

(1) In an enameled pan over low heat, stir together the cream and buttermilk or yogurt.
(2) Heat to just above body temperature (about 100° F.).
(3) Remove from heat, cover with plastic wrap, and allow to remain at room temperature overnight.
(4) The next day, a thickened, slightly

 INGREDIENTS

2 cups of whipping cream
4 tablespoons buttermilk or unflavored yogurt

tart, cream should have been created. Refrigerate. (Will keep for up to 2 weeks.)

INDEX

A

Appetizers 24
Apple Corer-Wedger 17
Apple Peeler/Corer/Slicer 12
Apple Tackle 12
Apples
    Antique Apple Mystique 4
    Cinnamon Candy Stewed
        Apples 79
    Poached Apples with
        Brandy Sabayon 86
Applesauce
    Sour Cream and
        Mustard Applesauce 38
    Early Transparent
        Applesauce 37

B

Baked Apple with Raspberries 96
Barbecue Sauce
    Cider Barbecue Sauce 47
Bars
    Date and Apple Bars 81
Beans
    Church Supper Baked
        Beans with Bacon Lattice
        Topping 56
Beverages 22

Bisque
    Autumn Squash and
        Apple Bisque 32
Bratwurst
    Smoked Bratwurst with
        Sauerkraut and Apples 39
Breads
    Apple Walnut Whole
        Wheat Bread 76
    Bacon Apple Cheddar
        Corn Sticks 65
    Caraway and Apple
        Rye Bread 68
    Caramelized
        Apple Gingerbread 92
    Whole Wheat
        Applesauce Bread 75
Breads and Muffins 65

C

Cabbage
    Braised Red Cabbage and
        Chestnuts 58
Carrots
    Gingered Carrots and Apples ... 60
Celery
    Scalloped Celery with
        Apples and Onions 61

Chedder
    Bacon Apple Cheddar
        Corn Sticks 65
    Cheddar Puffs 74
Chestnuts
    Braised Red Cabbage and
        Chestnuts 58
Chicken
    Roast Chicken with Loveage 40
Cider
    Autumn Cider and
        Champagne 23
    Hot Buttered Cider and
        Rum 22
Coleslaw
    Coleslaw with Cheddar
        Cheese and Apples 62
Compote
    Warm Compote of
        Winter Fruits 100
Cookies
    Chewy Apple and
        Pecan Cookies 83
Cooking Apples 9
Corer with Wooden Plunger 20
Corn
    Bacon Apple Cheddar
        Corn Sticks 65
Crème
    Crème Fraíche 105
Crescents, Chunks, and Dice 18
Crusts
    Old-Fashioned Pie Crust 94

D, E
Desserts 78
Duckling
    Autumn Roast Duckling with
        Apples 52
Dumplings
    Apple Dumplings 77
Eating Apples 2

F, G
Food Mill 21
Frosting
    Maple Cream Cheese
        Frosting 78
Gingerbread
    Caramelized Apple
        Gingerbread 92
Gravy
    Bourbon Pan Gravy 45

H
Ham
    Braised Ham in an Apple
        Wine Cream Sauce 48
Harvest Butter 105
Herb-Infused Olive Oil 101
Herbed Vinegar 102

I, J
Ice Cream
    Apple Lavender and Lemon
        Thyme Ice Cream 91

Apples and Brown
　Sugar Ice Cream 90
Jelly
　Lavender and Scented
　　Geranium Jelly 104
　Rosemary and
　　Nasturtium Jelly 103

L

Lamb
　Acorn Squash Stuffed with
　　Lamb and Curry 42
Lemon Sauce 78
Liver
　Chicken Liver Pâté with
　　Apples 24
　Mark's Liver and
　　Apple Canapés 28
Loaves
　Bacon Apple
　　Sourdough Loaves 72
　French Loaves 70

M, N, O

Main Dishes 39
Muffins
　Cracked Wheat and
　　Apple Muffins 66
National Apple Register of the United
　　Kingdom 3
Omelets
　Apple Pecan Camembert
　　Omelet 35

Blue Cheese Omelet with
　Apples and Walnuts 34

P

Pancakes
　Apple Pancake 89
　Oven Apple Pancake (French
　　Clafoutis) 88
Pâté
　Chicken Liver Pâté with
　　Apples 24
Pear-Corer 19
Peas
　Tailgate Pea Soup with
　　Apples 30
Pies
　Apples and
　　Raisin Brown Sugar Pie 84
　Old-Fashioned Pie Crust 94
Pork
　Crown Roast of Pork with
　　Apple Sausage Dressing 44
　Oven-Barbecued
　　Pork Tenderloins 50
　Pork Chops with Apples and
　　Bacon 46
Potatoes
　Potato Soup with
　　Cheddar Cheese and Apple ... 33
Pudding
　Esther's Ozark Pudding 80
　Apple and Cranberry
　　Bread Pudding 82

Puff Pastry
    No-Fail Puff Pastry 95

R, S, T

Ribs
    Country Style Ribs 51
Rumakis
    Apple Tempura Rumakis 26
Sabayon Sauce 87
Salads
    Baby Garden Green Salad 63
    Coleslaw with
      Cheddar Cheese and Apples .. 62
    Sesame Shrimp and
      Apple Salad 64
Sauerkraut
    Smoked Bratwurst with
      Sauerkraut and Apples 39
Sausage
    Apple Breakfast Sausage 36
Scones
    Cinnamon Apple Scones 67
Shrimp
    Sesame Shrimp and
      Apple Salad 64
Smith Myth 7
Soups
    Autumn Squash and
      Apple Bisque 32
    Potato Soup with
      Cheddar Cheese and Apple ... 33
    Tailgate Pea Soup with
      Apples 30

Sourdough
    Bacon Apple Sourdough
      Loaves 72
    Sourdough Starter 73
Spirals, Rings, and Rainbows 16
Squash
    Acorn Squash Stuffed with
      Lamb and Curry 42
    Autumn Squash and
      Apple Bisque 32
Sweet Potatoes
    Gratin of Apples, Sweet
      Potatoes and Onions 59
Tarts
    Apple Tart 97
    Apple Tart with
      Walnuts in a Puff Pastry 98
Tea
    Lemon Verbena and
      Apple Peel Tea 22

V

Vanilla Sugar 101
Vegetables 58
Venison
    Cider-Marinated
      Venison Roast 54
Vinegars and Jellies 101

Traditional Country Life Recipe Books from
BRICK TOWER PRESS

Forthcoming Titles

Clambake
Cranberry Companion
Pumpkin Companion

American Chef's Companion
Chocolate Companion
Fresh Herb Companion
Thanksgiving Cookery
Victorian Christmas Cookery

For More Information on Apple Companion:

Liz Clark teaches cooking in her restored antebellum home on the bluffs above the Mississippi River in historic Keokuk, Iowa. To request a newsletter of her upcoming classes, call Southeastern Community College at 800-344-7045.

Applesource ships a wide range of apple varieties from late October to early January. For a brochure, call 800-588-3854 or write to the following address: Applesource, Tom & Jill Vorbeck, Rt. 1, Chapin, IL 62628

The North American Fruit Explorers (NAFEX), a non-profit organization, is a good source for information on apple varieties and home fruit culture. For membership information, write to NAFEX, Rt 1, Box 94, Chapin, IL 62628, (Jill Vorbeck is membership chair.)

MAIL ORDER AND GENERAL INFORMATION

Many of our titles are carried by your local book store or gift and museum shop. If they do not already carry our line please ask them to write us for information.

If you are unable to purchase our titles from your local shop, call or write to us.
Our titles are available through mail order. Just send us a check or money order for $9.95 per title with $1.50 postage to the address below or call us Monday through Friday, 9 AM to 5PM, EST. We accept Visa and Mastercard.

Send all mail order, book club, and special sales requests to the address below or call us for a free catalog. We would like to hear from you.

E-mail: bricktower@aol.com

Internet Bookstore: (ebooks-info@access.digex.net)
order number 12203 for the electronic edition
P12203 for the print edition

Brick Tower Press
1230 Park Avenue, 10th Floor
New York, NY 10128

Telephone & Facsimile
1-212-427-7139
1-800-68-BRICK